Aging Gracefully with Dignity, Integrity & Spunk Intact: Aging Defiantly

Including Ten Tips to Keep People Off Your Back

NORMA ROTH

authorHOUSE®

AuthorHouse™
1663 Liberty Drive
Bloomington, IN 47403
www.authorhouse.com
Phone: 1-800-839-8640

First published by AuthorHouse 12/17/2009

ISBN: 978-1-4389-6432-4 (sc)
ISBN: 978-1-4490-2101-6 (hc)

Printed in the United States of America
Bloomington, Indiana

This book is printed on acid-free paper.

Come take my hand in yours
remember yourself, the self of dreams
Renew those quests
temper them with wisdom (and maturity)
and take hold of that silver ring
and go with it …

Norma Roth

CONTENTS

PART I

Preface

The art of aging gracefully is what this book is about, not the agony; the joys of growing older, not the fears and panic; the wonders that are on the horizon, not the inevitable. For this new dynamic Silver Generation may well be at the vanguard of an incredible age never before seen in the history of the world, with assists from the worlds of medicine and science that might seem like magic. For this new and dynamic generation marching into the twenty-first century, a new world awaits.

Some years back, I started to think about writing a piece on aging gracefully and avoiding the hang-ups and the no-good-doers, who seem to be out there giving a large assist to the growing population of grey-haired adults marching down the path to senility and other diminishing capacities associated with aging, when a friend of mine asked me for advice. "How can this be?" she moaned. "I can't seem to remember things, I don't know where I put things, I can't find things, I am really worried. Am I getting old? Is this the scourge of old age creeping up on me?" I figured she must have asked me because she knew and liked and trusted me, or because I was a good decade older than her, and who, if not I, would take what she was saying seriously and treat her kindly? My friend is a good, kind, intelligent human being, and she was clearly in pain. Quickly, I tried to assure her with a very positive "Of course not!" In fact, I had already started thinking about the warnings of diminishing faculties. After all—I was sixty! I had begun to suspect, too, that many of these fears might be hogwash. So I asked another question my mind had been playing with. "How long have you been putting things where you can't find them?" I asked. Surprised, she responded a bit sheepishly, "Well, truthfully, maybe, for a long time ... you don't think?"

Her voice trailed off. Quickly, I took the opportunity to ask still another question. "And how many times in your life," I asked, "have you walked into a room and not known why you were there?" "Oh," she replied, "that too ... I must really be in early senility—do you think?" "No, I definitely do not," I replied, rather sharply, finding myself increasingly agitated. Calming down, I said with as much definitiveness as I could, "I think you have been doing that most of your life—maybe it is happening a bit more than before." And I added another thought that had been developing for a while: "Maybe you're noticing it more, that's all; perhaps it is exaggerated by the dire warnings of a society that contemplates every aspect about itself and is seriously afraid of growing older." Now, I was really into it, and telling her I wanted to think more about the subject, I added, assuredly, that I believed she and our contemporaries had major resources not yet used and would find ways to draw upon them. I promised to send her some material on the subject.

Since then, I have thought often about this question of aging gracefully "with dignity, integrity, and spunk intact," and because I have come to believe that this new and rapidly emerging group "entering that age" will have to forge its own way, I feel this new generation will have to move ahead not only with a great deal of spunk but with defiance as well if they are to have the life they want, the life they are entitled to, and in fact, the life that seems there for the taking. I have taken a closer look at social and psychological attitudes about aging as well as pharmaceutical and real estate interests, and taken note of the vast amounts of advertisements, many of which invite the elderly to maintain "independent" living by moving into "care facilities" (which may seem to some to be an oxymoron) before the "scourge" of aging grabs them and they lose their faculties, or even move on to dementia and the Alzheimer's road.[1]

I have noticed, too, that this obsessive focus on the deterioration of the elderly (or as I prefer to call them, the "Silver Generation") often overlooks a vital factor. Through the modern miracles of science and medicine, this emerging generation will have longevity and health never before seen in the history of the world. In other words, they are, and will continue to be, a dynamic generation well into their eighties—or even nineties. Yes! Through diet, exercise, and medical attention, they will live longer, remaining alert and active, and may well achieve great things. Given the knowledge and experience base of what has come to be referred to as a highly overeducated, overachieving group, this new Silver Generation may be surprisingly productive once they become cognizant of their potential, take charge of their lives, and chart their own course.

My hypothesis then, which started to develop some years ago—and continues strongly—is that the negativity and fear of old age being focused upon today do not fit the rapid development of technological discoveries that are resulting in warding off the signs of aging. In fact, the attitudes of this society and the consequent concerns of the newly growing group entering that age are out of proportion to reality. In short, I am now of the opinion that a great many of the fears and tremors about this Silver Generation are, indeed, hogwash!

One recent example is illustrative: A cousin of mine in her early eighties was recently forced to sell a magnificent home on an island near Los Angeles, where she and her husband had spent the last fourteen

---

1   This book focuses on normal changes that occur in aging where science and medicine are predicting what many older people have discovered—that the brain can remain relatively healthy and functional throughout life. Alzheimer's disease and senile dementia are outside of the discussion in this book. They are considered progressive and degenerative, leading to severe impairments.

years. Because of health problems (her husband could no longer drive and, unfortunately, she did not), their growing dependency on others, and their isolation as well as increasing physical problems, they had to sell their home. The burden of the move fell on my cousin. One day, a member of her family, undoubtedly thinking that he was being observant, made the unkind comment that she, my cousin, was losing her short-term memory. Confronting her husband and lifelong partner, she asked his opinion: He told her, kindly, that he may have noticed a bit of that. A realist and well-educated, my cousin immediately arranged for a doctor's appointment and was ready to start therapy; she had read about exercises that were working with short-term memory loss when she wrote me. I quickly wrote back an angry letter telling her what I thought of the unkind remark of her relative—but I told her more. Certainly, I suggested that she not miss her physician's appointment, but I ventured my opinion that, given the circumstances—a big move from a large paradise she had known for so long; the anticipation of having to adjust to a new home on the East Coast (winters in New England do not generally bring a smile to anyone's face, unless they ski); having to sort through more than a few decades of acquisitions, while having to face the fact that her husband was in failing health—I would not be surprised if good old "stress" might just be the culprit behind her supposed short-term memory failure.

After a short while, she sent me a note: "How could you have known?" The words jumped off the page. Her doctor had told her the same exact thing I had. I began to think that I should pull together the empirical data I had gathered over the last decade (maybe a small sampling, it is true, but what did Freud have, after all?). In no time flat, I had several chapters outlined and so much more to say.

Putting aside the severe medical aspects of aging problems like Alzheimer's disease and senile dementia, which are degenerative diseases requiring special attention, I have come to the conclusion, indeed, that a great deal of the warnings about aging, the signs we should look for, the embarrassments those entering that age often feel, are part medical, part psychological—and a lot of hogwash. I am firmly of the opinion, not as a medical person, or psychiatrist, or specialist, but as an intelligent, thoughtful, independent scholar, that these attitudes and theories of brain drain are, in fact, caused in great part by the attitudes of others. In other words, outmoded social attitudes and behavior in large part are leading this Silver Generation down an un-merry path. In fact, continuing to collect my own data, I believe that too much of the "going-down-the tubes" mentality toward aging plays on fears, apprehensions, and panic unnecessarily, while depleting the energy and attention that would better be used to focus on planning for an active, participatory lifestyle and more, which may well lie in wait for those entering that age.

Every day, wherever I am, I find more and more examples supporting my hypothesis: When I go for a medical exam, administrators and nurses near retirement age share their desire to travel, to learn new things, to pick up things that they had started and want to continue doing—but also share their fears and concerns about encroaching older years and their ability to do all this: to move about, to travel, to maintain their mental acuity, to keep their wits. They must, I am convinced, talk to me because they note on my charts my infamous birth date and know I must share their concerns. Mostly, their concerns are more oriented to the loss of mental faculties than physical, probably because of the many technological developments in this new century that are more publicized. This age already offers some replacement parts, and by mid-century—or even before that—it will undoubtedly offer more "bionic-like" replacement parts for much of our body hardware like wrists and joints; these changes are limitless and dynamic in terms of improving potential lifestyles and quality of life.

Other stories unfold too: One longtime friend is annoyed with herself because she was at the vanguard of computers and let it go … and doesn't know if, at seventy, she can move ahead with it at her age. But with a little bit of encouragement, I am certain she will quickly pick it up again (with the enormous boost of muscle memory, perhaps—that part of us that remembers things like playing an instrument even if we haven't played it for many years), and will be able to continue her learning—acquired so far in advance of her time by sheer curiosity and mental attitude—and resume her teaching of others what does not come as easily as it still does to her.

Another friend has just put together an incredible photography book: photographs she has taken in the last few years hiking in the Western mountains (she is also in her seventies and had been motivated by her project to get into physical shape so she could hike in those mountains, and she did). Last year, I heard a modern piece composed for the horn player of the Boston Symphony Orchestra. The composer was in the audience; he had come up from New York to hear the performance (he is ninety-nine). I would suspect that he, like many members of the growing Silver Generation, subscribes to the "Use It or Lose It" theory—another area that modern medicine and science are seriously entertaining as a means for continuing maximum use of mental faculties. Simply stated, the theory posits the early findings that those who continue to use their brain retain its use; those who do not, lose it. Consider the ramifications of this powerful finding, particularly for the Silver Generation.

This book invites readers "entering that age" to take another look at what is really going on and enables new, growing, and already dynamic members of the Silver Generation at the forefront of a new age of health and resources to take a more realistic approach to their lives; to draw and build upon their strengths; to ignore, for the most part, their weaknesses; and to chart a new course. This generation can not only take control of their own lives, but can also fully participate in the world around them.

In addition, I have also come to believe that there is a source of wealth already existing within each individual, waiting to be retrieved, as well as undeveloped resources ready to be tapped. Once realized, the rich resources already existing will play a major part in the lives of this generation. This enlightened generation may well find they are losing far less than they thought, and may, in fact, be gaining a bright new world; at least, with diligence, perseverance, stubbornness, creativeness, and sometimes defiance—this Silver Generation does not have to lose this one.

Part I of this book deals with discussions of existing cultural attitudes and behavior patterns toward those entering that age that are negative and life-altering, and focuses upon debunking a fair number of myths involving social attitudes toward their lifestyle that are not in sync with scientific, medical, and technological advances. The excessive concerns and panic felt by those entering that age can be fairly easily handled through methods and techniques such as compensation, and they need not present insurmountable obstacles. In short, Debunking Myths gives advice on how to handle the myriad anxieties that often occur unnecessarily in those entering this age at the first sign of what is considered irreversible aging.

Part II of this book is dedicated to assessing strengths and weaknesses and exploring treasures within the self, existing resources which may have been started and stopped, things that you may have wanted to do but didn't, that you may have tried, but did not become as proficient at as you may have liked to, or somehow did not pursue—life got in the way. Further, Part II explores a potential base of stored knowledge within the self that consists of much of life's knowledge that was learned well, as well as experience and more, which I have called the Personal Retrieval System (PRS). I believe, in view of recent scientific research and an educational system that stresses a pedagogy of continual learning and relearning, testing and reinforcing over the years, this knowledge is not only stored within each of us, but can easily be accessed. As a new world unfolds, and science opens new pathways to stored memory banks within the self, it will serve this new dynamic Silver Generation well in the years to come. This age already holds the promise of long life and health—and now is rapidly moving toward rediscovering and retrieving learned and stored knowledge. Part II also deals with empowerment as a tool to minimize unnecessary hurdles that would further seek to impede growth and independence of those entering that age. Through empowerment and aging defiantly, this new generation will be able to further overcome societal constraints and better chart its own course. Adopting a new paradigm modeled after the continuous learning system that has been part of most of our lives (since the age of five and still continuing), and juxtaposing the wonders of medicine and science, the amazing potential of this new generation is explored. The journey looks to be an exhilarating and dramatic one into uncharted territory, in which this dynamic new Silver Generation will be at the forefront. This dynamic generation has an opportunity to be the leaders and pathfinders in an age that presents the most amazing life-extending potential in the history of the world.

The art of growing older with dignity, integrity, and spunk intact, and aging defiantly, is what this book is about: the art, not the agony; the joys of growing older, not the fears and panic. For this generation, in this new century, may well be at the vanguard of what may be an incredible output never before seen in the history of the world, assisted by an era of medical, scientific, and technological gifts that will bring limitless opportunities to those willing to take the risk. Vast resources lie at their disposal for combating and dealing with yesterday's concept of "aging," both physical and mental. Vast resources lie, too, within the self, waiting to be retrieved. For this new and dynamic generation marching into the twenty-first century, a new world awaits, and this author truly believes it merely waits to be explored. It can be a wonderful and awe-inspiring journey and one not to be missed.

Chapter 1

ENTERING THAT AGE![2]

I found myself in conflict with the so-called social posture that asks me to accept loss of brainpower as an inevitable part of entering that age; I could not help becoming more suspicious of the "this-is-the-way-it-is, accept-it" societal attitude: How could I accept it when a whole lifetime of learning and expectation—of doing— was a driving force in my life? I found myself face to face with a need to test this theory: Science is at the forefront of opening up pathways to memory that have not been understood before, suggesting that pathways to long-term memory may be available throughout our lifetime, while medicine and research support a host of wonderful life-enhancing possibilities. Given the current stage of science, medicine, and technology, and the educational process to which I had been subjected, the concept of a storage retrieval system within the brain that could be retrieved and accessed was not too much of a stretch. I found myself with a strong need to test this concept—given the alternative.

---

2   By which I mean anywhere from fifty-five-plus where our present-day society singles you out or you identify yourself as of that age past active and full participation in the world around you; where you begin to think that you are no longer a vital part of your world as you used to be, where you feel that "winding down" is what you ought to be doing, when you are made to feel that some of those great plans you had are no longer in reach, that living everyday life is simply enough of a burden—most of which I label "hogwash."

I have finally reached the point where it is all coming together. When I was young, there was so much to learn: every day, new adventures; every day, new thoughts; every day, new facts. I felt as though I were truly a blank slate or a sponge. As a slate, so much was being written; as a sponge, I could not soak up enough of the multitude of data and experiences surrounding me. Something was always out of reach. It would have been a whole lot easier if I had fewer interests, but I was not discerning. I wanted to know it all. I labored to learn everything that was given to me to study. I spent fruitful and fruitless hours studying all of the subjects put before me. Fruitful because of the wonderful world of learning I was engaged in; fruitless because of the incessant forgetting and relearning factor (or so I thought at the time).

The educational process in New York City, where I attended the public schools (probably similar to many other public schools throughout this country), was geared at that time to repeating the same things over and over again until some point was reached when our instructors were satisfied the material had been learned and put in some safe storage bank in our brain, convinced that the information could be retrieved at will—forever. (Computer technology had not yet entered the world we lived in, or I firmly believe the nomenclature would have been different: brain cells, data bases, retrieval systems, and so on.)

So we learned and were tested, and we learned and were tested, and one need only remember the introduction on a hit record by Peter, Paul, and Mary in the seventies, where in explaining the song to come, Peter Yarrow described the methodology used in the song's lyrics the group was about to sing as the basic instructive method of every single child's song—that is, "repetition," the major methodology of the early educating process. Throughout the educational departments in the vast arsenal of schools, that methodology did, indeed, revolve around that philosophy—or pedagogy, as it was called. Why else would the educational process repeat the same information and data over and over, if not for a firm belief that through repetition, the information would finally seep into the recesses of the mind, where it could be drawn upon in later years? That there was a method to the madness, I never questioned. Incessant forgetting was a supreme insult to the intelligence and would not be tolerated. Information could be learned in such a manner that what was being taught—or most of it—would never be forgotten: if we paid attention, if we studied, if we truly wanted to learn. Therefore, diligently—oh, so diligently—educators drilled us and taught all of us the same things over and over again, and from time to time, we wondered where their minds were.

Somehow, I got the message, and as I got older, I relied on that base. As a student in elementary school, high school, and even college, I studied whatever was assigned—overkill, to be sure—but I so enjoyed revisiting the material I really liked so much, like literature, poetry, bits of science, history, philosophy, and even math. I loved literature the best, I think, because I could enter different worlds—worlds that seem to have remained with me all my life. I have often thought that if the pedagogy were correct, constant repetition would have left me with a great wealth of literature stored somewhere in my mind, not yet fully utilized, to be drawn upon at a later period in my life.

I remember reading about two men who did wondrous things: One, tucked away in Tunisia during World War II, wrote a definitive historical work using the resources of his mind, since he had no library with him—it was an age of burning of books; the other, Primo Levi, locked in a camp, was asked by an inmate to teach him Italian. He did that the best way he knew how: by teaching him the Italian language

13

through parts of that awesome work we all know as Dante's *Inferno*. Most memorable to me was that this magnificent work of great literature was tucked away in Levi's brain. "Tucked away" is the key expression that suggested to me a retrieval system in the mind of stored information, and further, it indicated there it would remain (barring serious disorders), perhaps for a lifetime, wanting and waiting for opportunities to be retrieved.

I do not profess to be a Primo Levi, but as I approached sixty, on my own level, I remember feeling a little like that regarding my own knowledge base. At fifty, I began to think, along with lifelong friends, that we of the seemingly overeducated generation might have our own libraries—our personal storehouses of knowledge and experience. I was finding, for myself, I no longer needed to run to the library, or the computer, or indeed do the incessant library research. I seemed to have a knowledge base of my own that I could draw on, where I apparently had stored facts and data of sufficient interest and importance to me.

When I reached the age of maturity—whenever that was—I no longer had to start to work through a deep concept and stop so many times to first either read a dozen more books or look up an equal number of concepts and facts before I dared to approach the subject matter. I am glad to say I did not feel bereft of a knowledge base to help me develop my thinking. I could, at long last, reach for it and utilize my personal storehouse of knowledge, experience, and expertise to draw on, grapple with, and reach out toward some broader (and perhaps original) conclusions of my own. Past family life, almost past professional obligation, what I began to seek most of all, I think, was to start putting it all together—those many thoughts and concepts and ideas and theories that I have played with for almost a lifetime.

Suddenly, all things seemed "Go" for the deeper exploration into the areas of great interest to me! Ah! There's the rub ...

So, at the very moment (well, a decade or so later) when I am—as many of you are—finally ready (or so it seems: age, education, experience, and travel entering into the equation too), life offers the supreme hurdle: The mental and emotional afflictions of the "aging process" come into play—or so we are told! And we stand to lose all the wealth gathered over a lifetime. Everyone within our circles assures us, seems to warn us, to shout at us, that we are bound to be afflicted with—and most probably will not be able to stop—the aging process! "It's simple," they say. "This is the way it is: We grow old, we lose cells—and with it—our minds cease to be reliable." That is a fact of life! And who am I to dispute such absolutes?

Well...not so fast: Entering that stage, it is hard—and incongruous—to face a seemingly societal certainty that states so emphatically that at the precise moment in time when I (and so many of my friends and colleagues) am ready to bring it all together, to think seriously about all the bits and pieces that have been working their way through my mind all these years on myriad themes, I should be faced with the prospect of confronting the aging process and inevitable and permanent memory loss.

The irony of it does not escape me, nor the senselessness of it all, nor the absurdity of all absurdities, nor the sense that this may be the cruelest blow of my life—if true. But, I find, I am faced with serious doubts regarding the truthfulness of these statements. It seems paradoxical, especially for a member of a dynamic new century, to be told that after all this learning, over a lifetime, the information will not be available to me—will actually be unavailable to me! To be robbed of such enormous potential, epic in its proportion, seems tragic—especially if it is unnecessary—to be robbed of a productive life and achievement is simply not acceptable on so many different grounds.

It occurs to me that the societal attitudes concerning this newly developing group, this Silver Generation, are overlooking vital factors that absolutely fly in the face of the promise of medical, scientific, and technological output pushing in an opposite direction. Modern miracles of science and medicine predict this emerging generation will have longevity and health never before seen in the history of the world—all kinds of wonders coming our way with the potential to make this generation's life glitter and sparkle, not dim and disappear. According to science, medicine, and technology, the changes expected are dramatic and, some would say, fantastic: especially for this dynamic generation expected to live (and live well) into their eighties—or even nineties (evidence of which is already around us).

Thinking back to those old school days, and remembering how much of my time was spent relearning what I had already learned, I could not help also becoming even more suspicious of the "this-is-the-way-it-is, accept-it" societal attitude. How could I accept it when a whole lifetime of learning and expectation—of doing—was a driving force in my life? The Renaissance Woman has been my goal, not a feeble person losing her mind. I started, then, to seriously consider how much of the pedagogy of yesteryear might be applicable to the present dilemma that my generation and I were finding ourselves stumbling over as we entered that age.

The possibility of a hoax[3] being perpetrated on me started to ferment. In particular, the fears and concerns about learning or remembering substantive areas, and the uncertainly of intelligently discussing or writing about academic areas of the past, stood in sharp contrast with the potential for remembering things, purposely and dutifully and diligently taught throughout life, as well as the rapid advancements in science and medicine. It also presented an obstacle of gigantic proportions to me personally in regard to works like Proust's *Remembrance of Things Past* and all the other great works of literature that were long, complex, and cumbersome, which I had held in such reverence expecting to be read exactly at this later time in my life.

I started to do a great deal more thinking about the so-called aging process vis-à-vis the educational experience of learning, learning/forgetting, losing/gaining. Obviously, I realized there was much to think about regarding the relationship of the learning process to which we had been exposed to the so-called social theories of aging. And I began to get a definite sense that society might indeed be perpetrating a hoax on me and on those of my generation who looked forward to entering that age, to the wonderful gifts that might well lie in store for us. And that society might just be wrong!

I became intrigued with gathering data and thinking about those data bases that we, as adults, had acquired (or thought we had), the loss of which we would not take lightly as an expected result of the aging process. I could not easily accept an attitude that glibly implied that

3   I define "hoax" as something that others try to put over on you as being an ab-solute that leaves little or no room for argument; however, it does not stand on firm footing. It props itself up as seeming to have a great deal of foundation and support, but like a house built of straw (as we all know from our fairy tale days), once investi-gated, the structural support crumbles: in other words, what is being touted as final and absolute is in reality *full of sound and fury signifying nothing.* One of the diction-ary definitions of hoax is "malicious deception"—need I say more?

retaining complex thoughts and theories, those weighty substantive areas we learned and memorized and regurgitated and stored, was a losing game. I also knew intuitively that the "baby boomer" generation just a bit behind us, who were breaking all records in the way things are supposed to be (and aging in particular), would continue to do so when they entered that age. I knew they would not tolerate this outworn social attitude for one moment, now, would they? I knew, too, they would break any barriers that would diminish their right to remain "young" forever: A theory of diminishing brainpower would be to them, as it suddenly appeared to me, unacceptable! Not for them and not for this dynamic Silver Generation. Too much on the horizon; too many hopes and plans; too much life yet to be lived!

I found myself face to face with a need to test this concept of a storage retrieval system with the brain based on current scientific studies and the learning process to which most of us had been exposed. I understood intuitively that to test the theory of a personal data bank at this point, given all the fears and horror stories the Silver Generation is subjected to, the desire might not be a high priority on the list for those entering that age. To enter on a journey to potentially undiscovered talent that had not been used for years, and further, to test the principle of a retrieval system, might not be welcome. What courage that might take, what arrogance, too, to embark upon a line of thought that considered a storage system within the brain that could be accessed, retrieved, and utilized for a lifetime perhaps. In other words, a search for expansion of brainpower rather than brain loss would be a far-out reach, perhaps, for accessing data that had not been utilized for decades!

Would my generation, would I, want to open myself up to allow others to see me struggling with yet another attempt to remember, when I might be having trouble remembering even the basics? Or put another way—would that journey simply be too embarrassing? The disappointment, I realized, would not be only to the others, but really to myself! And, in my heart of hearts, perhaps there was the fear that if I failed, I might put one more pin in what might be a growing body of alleged observational data by obsessed friends and family to which I was not immune. I might come to believe that I was losing it. However, it was also incredibly hard for me to believe that all that earlier education, studying, and teaching methodology (barring serious degenerative diseases like Alzheimer's or senile dementia) was a waste. I was reminded of the inspiring words of one of my truly favorite poets, Robert Frost: "I took the road less traveled," he said, "and that has made all the difference." And then there were all of the drives of science, medicine, and technology!

I decided to go on this journey. Because, what if that earlier educational system and newer scientific theories were true? What if, with a little practice, I could remember things thought to be long forgotten: places, events, books, themes, characters, lines—beautiful lines—of favorite poetry. What if I could? If those entering that age could but tap into inner resources, reach an inner recess of the mind—all those bits of information we incessantly put into our own data base (our minds) that might be sitting and waiting for us to retrieve: What joy! The possibilities were endless to contemplate, the journey too inviting not to make.

A new paradigm based on learning, relearning, reinforcing—learning, relearning—over and over again until satisfied that reinforced, it was learned, and would be remembered and be retained and be able to be recalled (accessed) was in order. A cumulative process for sure must have as its endpoint the ability to retrieve a whole lot of information. The implications of that broad-based educational system for this dynamic, new, very well-educated generation were exhilarating to consider. Certainly, the reality of our educational system—and the continuation of those methods (diligently learned) throughout our lifetime—strongly suggested that our learning, relearning, and reinforcing might not have been a vain gesture. Certainly, the scientific and medical promise of longevity, health, and more demanded a new paradigm better suited to the times, to the reality, and to the demands of the Silver Generation.

Who can argue that our dynamic, new older generation would not greatly benefit from and be far ahead of most people on tapping into these resources, since how could it be denied that, by sheer weight of age, our accumulation of a knowledge base, our experience, is not larger than younger groups of people?

Franklin Delano Roosevelt said so long ago, when our country was in a terrible time, "This generation ... has a rendezvous with destiny." This statement, though meant for a different time and situation, holds a message of worth for members of the Silver Generation in this new twenty-first century. FDR did not say we were defeated, or that the battle was too hard, but that with effort, we would prevail! Of course, he was talking about the Great Depression. We are talking about a new generation with tremendous possibilities to leave potentially great achievements behind for the next generation. Given the current problems of this era, the message seems apt for those entering that age.

So as you enter that age, think not about closing down your talents and resources but of delving into that beautiful mind and brain that has taken in so much of life's experience, maybe more—much more than you think. What exciting possibilities might be on the horizon for this generation? Yes, this Silver Generation may well be in the vanguard with possibilities that seem endless.

So if you are still wondering if entering that age leads to a decline physically, mentally, and emotionally, you are asking the wrong questions. I suggest you should be asking these practical questions: Is it true? How true? And if true, can't it be overcome? Can't I learn to compensate? What about new resources? Can't they be moved faster? What can I do to maintain, retain, retrain? The answer to these questions, it seems to me, depends on who's looking.

I submit to the Silver Generation that the answers to these questions (both philosophical and practical) will determine how much of the world the Silver Generation may continue to lay claim to, whether members of this new dynamic group will be able to remain in charge of their own lives, and how much of that dynamic and active life this generation will have available to them to seek a newer world of their own making—the wonders of which seem almost magical. This book, then, is devoted to the goals and dreams of the Silver Generation, of the unlimited horizons of this new twenty-first century.

Chapter 2

DON'T PANIC:
THE SITUATION DEFINED

So you are having trouble remembering things? So you don't know where you put one item or another? So the thoughts you thought you were thinking slip away? DON'T PANIC. But when things happen to you, you get a queasy feeling in the pit of your stomach, and panic begins to set in. You ask yourself the question:

Is my life over? And then you take another look, a longer look—and ask yourself better questions: What is really going on here? Do I have the skills to cope? Can I handle it? And the real driving question: Will I be able to carve out the life I want as I enter that age rich with me: the goals and dreams I have, the potential that I want to explore, the ... and then you look at your support systems, and you will know the answer is a resounding YES!

So You Are Having Trouble

So you are having trouble remembering things? So you don't know where you put one item or another? So the thoughts you thought you were thinking slip away? DON'T PANIC! You look around sometimes and wonder where you were—your mind has wandered to another world or thought and you're not sure of what is being said or discussed around you. *DON'T PANIC!* You find you have put something in what you thought was a perfect spot and now you can't find it. Or you lose sight of a month or even a day ... is this Sunday or Monday? DON'T PANIC! But when things happen to you, you get a queasy feeling in the pit of your stomach, and panic begins to set it. You ask yourself the question: Is my life over? Will all that I want to learn be off-limits to me? Will all that I have learned go down the drain? Will all my plans for my grand achievements—the culminations of a lifetime—be frustrated? Will I spend my days in the endless pursuit of trying to find things; trying to remember names; trying to keep from burning down the house or taking too many or too few pills? Will the quality of my life deteriorate with the quality of my mind? Will I drift in and out and remember, in whiffs of clouds passing, the dreams I had after retirement, after the children have left the nest, of being creative, traveling, thinking, learning, maybe writing, or engaging in scintillating conversation? Or will I fail to remember even that? DON'T PANIC!

So you left a pot boiling on the stove? So you have looked for an hour and can't find your keys—again? So you can't remember why you came into this room, or that one, or ...? Time out! Is this the start of the disintegration and degeneration process that will start you on the road to that "long-term care" necessity? Or are some of these issues, like coming into a room and not knowing why you are there, simply an exaggeration of something that has been happening to you for a long time? Aren't you often looking for your keys? Aren't we all? Haven't you always looked for that or something of a similar nature? Yes, perhaps it is happening with more frequency, but isn't it rather a continuation of a pattern of behavior you have always had? It may well be, and you ought to pause to gain a bit of perspective.

Do you think it might be extremely difficult if you find yourself having trouble finding something or another, to designate specific places to put things and not deviate from those places? Of course you can do that! Do you think you won't be able to find your house keys or car keys if you leave them on the table by the door with an attractive key ring with your initials on it? I don't think so! Or regarding the situation of forgetting why you went into a room, do you think it might be too much trouble for you to go back down the stairs to the room where you had that thought that sent you up to the bedroom or den in the first place? (Good exercise, too!) Most of the time, you will remember! So now that you have begun to give a bit of thought to these so-called early indicators of that dreaded phase of entering that age, and seen they aren't that difficult to handle, is there anything stopping you from compensating for these very often troubling situations associated with entering that age?

Compensation is a technique for dealing with major issues presented in these several chapters on debunking myths and neutralizing panic. It is one of the most important of an arsenal of strong tools that will be introduced for you to bring to bear on the new situations you have encountered (and will continue to encounter) entering that age. Many of the studies I have read and the books and guides that are appearing on the horizon speak to the ability of those reaching a stage of forgetfulness to compensate for the situations in which this occurs. These are practical techniques, common sense, and not too difficult problem-solving techniques.

After you have tried and digested the techniques, which will be discussed fully in the chapters to come, you might want to take a moment to think about them! With a newly gained perspective, you will find yourself more and more capable—and fortified—to handle new situations and bring them under control. As you gain a different perspective, you will come to realize what is suggested to deal with the issues discussed will not be rocket science: You have the ability, you can use that ability, you can use it easily, and it is readily at your fingertips—no new skills needed. Many members of the Silver Generation are already discovering multiple innovative ways to rid themselves of these nuisances and seeming obstacles. I think you will find that these troubling concerns can be met with little effort, and that meeting the challenges they present will allow you to create a world in which you can participate more fully and on your own terms.

Remember: You have been around longer than this thing you are facing. How about using all the skills, the experiences, the ingenuity, the creativeness you have used all these many years (a half century or more!) to defeat this culprit? The very skills, talents, and abilities you used to become successful in life: in a profession, in a business, in parenting. "Which skills?" you ask. Well, take any of the professions or various other positions or household executive jobs you have held over the years—include parenting, where, whether you are male or female, you must have learned lots of skills for self-preservation and time-outs—and pull them all together. You do have the resources to defeat many of the issues concerned with growing older. Consider the alternative when you ask yourself the dreaded question: What do I do with the rest of my life? Then ask yourself the better question: What can I do to ward off the deficiencies of age?

What to do? In a nutshell: Deal with these issues like you have dealt with everything else in your life —pick yourself up and move on. These years, the silver years, should and can be expansive, glittering, and sparkling like silver drops glittering on the water towards the close of day that mesmerize you, even if you have to squint a bit. Think of those lyrics of that old Judy Garland number that you have known for most of your life: "Look for the silver lining." Except you needn't look too far, because the silver lining is all around you. Have faith in yourself.

Cultivate that positive attitude you meant to all your life—unless you are one of the lucky ones who are already blessed with one—and then remember to use it. Cultivate whatever your heart desires: In the end, as in the beginning, you make the difference in how you can travel through these silver years.

Remember, too, you have stronger allies than any other group of older people moving into those silver years—more advantages than any such group has had in the history of the world. Science, medicine, and technology are on your side and already hard in pursuit of means and methods that will provide you with the basis for a level of health that will allow you to grow older with dignity and integrity—and with far more than you can imagine. You are at the forefront of seeing rapidly developing technologies that will increase your life span and give you greater possibilities for both physical and mental health.

All kinds of new sciences are springing up: bioengineering, biomedical research, and biologically inspired engineering, which means that all the sciences are rushing to support this massive effort to move to uncover the secrets of extending life—and a healthy life at that. Architecture and engineering have joined the support system to enable what is also becoming known as the Age of Biology to move rapidly in the research and application of life-extending and life-enhancing technologies. And from the micro- and nano-biotechnological world, precise control of cells will become available too. Regarding increasing, improving, and repairing brain cell function, contrary to what has been thought, research is beginning to show that the brain may continue to generate new cells throughout life—yes, they may not die and decline from the age of thirty or forty, but actually regenerate. Further, neuroscience tells us that continuously challenging the brain with physical and mental activity helps maintain its structure and function.

The "Use It or Lose It" phenomenon is already being marketed, as company advertisements address mental workouts and games to improve memory and other means for compensating for some short-term effects of memory loss.

There is so much progress affecting both cell deterioration and physical deterioration, the world has begun to spin with limitless possibilities. A fascinating century is emerging. Take note of it! This is the right time for those entering those years to get on with life. Yes, it is time for you to prepare for a long and healthy life: It is time for you to chart your own course. It is time to learn the art of aging with dignity, integrity, and spunk, and when you need it, aging defiantly, and leave behind the fears of a society not yet in sync with you as you move into the twenty-first century—and dream those impossible dreams—with confidence that will enable your silver years to indeed be good ones for you as well as potentially limitless in possibilities. Look around you; they already are!

Recently, I have been amused to see little mechanical devices moving down the street at a quick pace. On second look, I see motorized chairs scooting at a pretty fast pace happily down the block. They almost give off an air of fun as they whiz by—they also say, "Watch out; watch me." Nothing more than specially redesigned wheelchairs for elderly mobility. In my neighborhood, they are helping to enable the elderly to remain living independent lives. High spirited as their mini-transit vehicles take them where they want to go, including shopping and restaurants—no slowing them down—each makes a statement: "I am not dropping out of the world, so move over!" I have made a mental note that when I get to that stage, that's how I will continue to get around: as independently as I possibly can. I told my doctor this many years ago; he laughed. He has retired before me; we live in the same neighborhood. I am of the firm opinion, when he can no longer get around on his own two feet, he will remember our conversation. And we will pass each other on the street as we whiz along on our electric vehicles. But first, I will do everything I can to maintain myself at high premium fitness—both physically and mentally—and start by taking notice of the amazing resources coming down the pike.

Look around you: You are already changing patterns of behavior by simply living active lives to a later age than ever in history. New pathways to maintain active, healthy lives spring up every day, allowing more and more options, and you know that! Exercise classes are being designed for you, nutritional tips to maintain energy, dermatological wonders to maintain looks. As you enter that age—especially as you enter that age—you are being encouraged to use both your body and brainpower, not coddle it!

Look around: This world—your world—is being radically altered by the new lives members of your Silver Generation are charting. I mentioned in the introduction the ninety-nine-year-old man who came to Boston to hear the Boston Symphony Orchestra play his newly composed piece. He was here again this year at one hundred to begin a birthday celebration in his honor with two adoring admirers, conductor James Levine and pianist Daniel Barenboim, both of whom, by the appearance of their schedules and activities, seem to have entered that age without taking much notice. Add that to a recent feature in *The New York Times* of a woman of ninety-three who wrote a cookbook for dining alone and liking it, with a picture of her in her small but well-equipped kitchen in New York, a candle-lit dinner on her table awaiting her, replete with an elegant wine goblet. Well, doesn't she deserve it? Don't you? And she is not alone. Didn't the first President

Bush parachute out of an airplane to celebrate his eightieth birthday? And, then again, at eighty-five?

Isn't Senator Byrd a marvel of a mind at the ripe age of ninety-one? Senator Byrd never ceases to amaze, and he seems to hold more wisdom as he carries around and quotes repeatedly and significantly from a copy of the Constitution, rattling off the historical background of the congressional legislation his far younger colleagues seem to have forgotten—or perhaps never knew. And don't be misled by those shaking hands turning the pages either: So he has Parkinson's disease. For many, that no longer seems a reason to opt out—not today! And if you are not convinced, pick up a copy of Senator Byrd's book on the last presidency: *Losing America: Confronting a Reckless and Arrogant Presidency*; how's that for confrontational and assertive? No intimidation force at work here. Aren't you just a bit embarrassed at the mental abilities he will not allow to fester? Undoubtedly, he is the personal embodiment of "use that brainpower or lose it": His cognitive ability is highly visible; his philosophical and constitutional outpourings are a testament to a mind in touch with all his resources, and a mind in touch with the world. What a role model he is; what a joy to see and hear those deep and penetrating arguments on the Senate floor. Certainly, the applications and admonition to those entering that age are exquisitely clear: Use your mind, continue to use your mind, and don't ever stop using your mind.

A few decades ago, Alvin and Heidi Toffler wrote a book entitled *The Third Wave*, in which they discussed what they predicted would be the next phase of society following the industrial society (which had replaced the agricultural one). They saw a movement back to the home base as a work place of the new century and described it as the Cottage Industry. I am not sure that the Tofflers had envisioned the dynamic changes of the late twentieth and early twenty-first centuries, including the new rise of the dynamic group I have called the Silver Generation. With the rapid developments of science and medicine in the fields of human biology, neurology, and engineering prolonging life span and health potential, the Cottage Industry stage seems particularly applicable to members of the Silver Generation. For those of you who have entered that age and want to continue working, but don't want to expend the energy or time traveling to and from work—or even working all the time—you will be doing nothing less than what the Tofflers predicted: setting up your cottage industries (working out of your homes). Many of you work out of your homes already.

If your wish is to continue professional work, that may well be available to you too. Many members of the Silver Generation are already doing this. As an attorney, I can tell you from first-hand experience I have not retired; hearings and conferences can now be had from the home base right across the country, and even on to Hawaii. Yes, a new age has come—and you are in a position to take advantage of it. Think of the ramifications for this dynamic new Silver Generation. I work the hours I please, at my own pace—and less and less, I must admit, as my interests take me in different directions. I take advantage of opportunities and engage in endeavors I never dreamed would be possible or open to me.

At this stage in your lives, I suspect many of you may well have a different idea of the kind of lifestyle you want, not the rocking chair overlooking a green pasture of another era. Many of you are determined to have an expanded version of what Robert Frost stated so eloquently as you move into this enormously challenging and limitless twenty-first century: "But I have promises to keep/And miles to go before I sleep/ And miles to go before I sleep." I believe this more closely reflects the attitudes and thoughts of many of you as you move into this enormously challenging and potentially limitless twenty-first century.

So the signs of longevity, longer life, and better health continue to mount; they appear all around you as this twenty-first century brings opportunities never before known in the history of the world. The Silver Generation is at the threshold of these major changes and is being given the opportunity to share in its wealth. So DON'T PANIC! There is so much you can do if you do not give in to that panic. So many things are working for those entering that age: The only limits may be the ones you create for yourself—so don't allow old concepts and old, outdated ideas to chart your course, and don't allow your experience, your wisdom, your expertise to go to waste. DON'T PANIC!

This world may well need the likes of this wiser generation to work through the mess we are currently in: You can and should spend your time more creatively and productively and wisely. Those who lived through the Great Depression have more skills, knowledge, and experience to help work through the most troublesome economic situation this world has seen since then—and wisdom as well. Factor that into this time and place.

There is no reason to deny that there are problematic areas that may be troublesome to those entering that age. There is no intent in this book to deny that the issues and concerns discussed exist as you enter that age (even if only an extension of what you have done all your life), but rather, it is the attempt to insinuate that these concerns are indicative of an active life that is coming to an end (yours!) that is the issue here. In fact, most of the concerns can be handled without great difficulty. In other words, you can deal with them!

The attitude and behavior that implies that your life is greatly diminished after you enter that age is out of proportion to the ability to deal with these issues in view of the dynamics of this century: your lifestyle, including your education and experience, and the mounting evidence of science and medicine as well. Most significantly, these issues are hardly insurmountable—hardly worth the obsessive concern. Therefore, the attitudes and behavior patterns that would see you closing up shop are not only wrong, but totally inappropriate in light of the lifestyle and knowledge base of the Silver Generation and the amazing fortification being provided by science, medicine, and technology. After considering the techniques and strategies in the forthcoming chapters, I believe that a better understanding of the dynamics to deal with the problems and concerns as you enter that age will enable you to feel more confident and secure as you chart your own course. You will also come to the conclusion that most of these concerns that had you panicked are indeed hogwash.

May I remind you again that it is the joy of aging that we are after, not the agony; the pleasure, not the pain. Some pain is unavoidable, but it can be compensable. You may have to knock over a few hurdles, but no one promised you a rose garden, now, did they? I deeply believe that you can make the difference in how you travel through your silver years: DON'T PANIC! Have that faith in yourself, get out those skills you have used all your life, take the lead, gain control over your life, and chart your individual course, and let no one else dare get in the way. These silver years are potentially far-reaching, full of glitter and sparkle. So get your act together, and join your peers in the most exciting venture of the twenty-first century: DON'T EVEN THINK OF PANICKING! It's a sheer waste of energy—YOURS! Your life deserves better.

Chapter 3

DEBUNKING MYTHS: DEFLECTING PANIC

Turning Problems of Aging on Their Head

Things you have done for much of your life may not seem to be working well; the things you gave no thought to seem to require excessive concentration; the fears and concerns you have heard about others now seem to loom before you; and you ask yourself how this will affect your life. The changes you note taking place in your behavior patterns need not signify the end of the world as you know it; they may merely mean you must change some of the ways you do things and develop some new techniques to meet new situations you are encountering. YOU CAN MANAGE IT!

Confronting Change

So you think your life is going awry because people are asking questions that make you feel uncomfortable; people you have known for years, and loved and trusted, are looking at you in a strange way, while you are finding, too, changes in your behavior that are leaving you unsettled, uncomfortable, and wondering about yourself. You don't like it one bit—but you don't know what to do about it either. The way you have done things much of your life may not seem to be working as well; the things you gave no thought to seem to require excessive concentration; the fears and concerns you have heard about others now seem to loom before you; and you can't help asking yourself the awful question of how this will affect your life—meaning your way of life as you have known it. Will it change it negatively? You fear that your freedom and independence of decision-making may be coming to an end.

This is a good time to remind you of the suggestion in the previous chapter, which basically boils down to—yes, you know—DON'T PANIC! Despite the advice, I do not doubt that many of you are feeling troubled about the questions raised here. Take heart. Help is on the way. The changes you note taking place in your behavior patterns need not signify the end of the world as you know it; they may merely mean you must change some of the ways you do things, and develop some new techniques to meet the new situations you are encountering.

Rest assured, you already possess many of the skills and abilities to adapt to these changes. Further, the allegedly "life-altering" phenomenon, the inevitability you have been led to believe you will encounter, may not, in fact, lead to the draconian results you fear.

Let's get specific and spend a few minutes really looking at and dissecting some of those allegedly powerful pitfalls to living a full life in these silver years, briefly discussed in the previous chapter: those signs of such alleged debilitation and waning of mental processes that (so you are told) must inevitably lead to—well, you know: assisted living quarters. Not because it is something you choose, but rather because you have been persuaded (falsely!) and pressured into believing that you no longer can live alone: You'll burn the house down, or lock yourself out of your home in the middle of the night, or search endlessly for something that should be right there—and so on.

Examining Three Areas of Concern
(Three Potential Panic Situations)

Let us examine these three concerns more closely:

> So you leave the water boiling on the stove?
> So you don't know where you put your keys?
> So you wonder why you came into this room
> in the first place?

So you leave the water boiling on the stove?

So you leave the water boiling on the stove and don't remember that you did it, if you leave the room? What to do? Run for help? Call for nursing assistance? Go into, heaven forbid, a nursing home? Think, for a moment: Would this happen if you had stayed in the kitchen? I doubt it! I very much doubt that if you stayed in the kitchen (especially kitchens being as small as they are these days), you would have failed to notice and remember that water was boiling on the stove and do whatever it is you might have wanted to do with that boiling water: make tea, boil eggs, boil pasta or rice—whatever. Simple suggestion number one: Don't leave a room, especially the kitchen, where you are doing chores, until you are done! Yes, that's all there is to this. You might be asking yourself: Why didn't I think of that? Right question!

Consider this more deeply: Why didn't you think of that? Perhaps because you have allowed yourself to accept the societal mores without questioning them? Or, because you have been conditioned into accepting these indicia as a sign of losing it? Because you bought into it: hook, line, and sinker? Think again: It is the wrong indicator of losing it, isn't it? It would be wrong to base the question of the necessity to change your entire lifestyle on that improper criterion, right? Hogwash! Merely because it is one of those totally acceptable societal constructs that you have never questioned doesn't mean it is fixed, unalterable, or correct.[4]

So the question that could be asked, the question that might make more sense to ask, the question or comment that would be kinder for a friend or relative to suggest, for instance, is whether you had realized that memory sometimes tricks one up at some age, and that it is so very easy simply not to do certain things like walk out of the kitchen when you have something on the stove.

Perhaps, if you were not so uptight about the way these infractions might appear to others now that you have entered that age, you might have thought of it yourself. Perhaps you are simply becoming more apt to forget you put that water on the stove at this point in your life than previously, even though, you might admit, this has happened throughout your life? Isn't it just that now you tend to do it more frequently? So what? Why don't so-called well-meaning friends and relatives make the right suggestions? Perhaps that is a question you should be asking yourself. Or, better still, just adopt this tried-and-true method and be done with it! Period!

Let's go on ...

---

4   As we go along, we will also consider comments and appropriate questions that might be made by friends and family members who want to be helpful and support-ive, instead of those uncomfortable comments, gestures, or raised eyebrows. If family and friends took the time to understand that natural changes occur throughout life, and that these particular ones that occur during this part of life are a natural, but not devastating, phenomenon, they might be more helpful. You will see as you continue through this chapter that these issues are not signs of such deterioration that others should be making assumptions of radical changes in your lifestyle as a result. Instead, the total social milieu could—and should, as you will realize—be made considerably more comfortable for those entering that age.

So you don't know where you put your keys?

Happening more often? Driving you crazy? Beginning to be downright embarrassing? Getting you uptight—becoming terribly aware of "eyes" following you and fixed looks on mouths forming those opinions of the entering-that-stage phenomenon you have reached in life? Try this strategy: DON'T PUT THINGS IN DIFFERENT PLACES than you have always put them—no matter how much better or safer or nearer you may think a new place might be, it isn't going to work! (The hardest part of this simple technique is the tendency for deviation: Even if you think you have found a better, more perfect place, DON'T DEVIATE!)

Put the d— thing where you always have. If you don't, you will find that you will be hiding it from yourself, and then have to go on a hunt, or try to reconstruct your steps that day—all the time getting more and more harried and disturbed and embarrassed as you rummage through this and that. If someone is waiting—AND WATCHING—well, you know what they are thinking, or you think what they are thinking, and it just puts that much more pressure on you as well. You start to fall into the self-flagellation routine: "How stupid of me, I had them just a minute ago," not to mention the embarrassment that is sure to creep in. Advice: Just use your old tried-and-tested places—always! And be done with it.

I'm sure some fastidious, organized people do this already from the get-go. (And there are such people who leave their keys to the house, keys to the door, keys to whatever, in exactly the same place all the time—and also in exactly the same pocket every single time. Yes, some people are creatures of habit; lucky them.) But for most of you, the suggestion above would probably be a welcome one—certainly more welcome than the embarrassment you may feel.

So the question that could be asked in this situation by friends or family members, the question that would be kinder to ask, the question that might make sense to ask, for instance, is whether you had considered always leaving your keys in the exact same place. And if these friends and family members meant to be kind, why didn't they ask just that? Or a friend might say, "I was reading and thought it a good idea ..." If he or she really wanted to be kind—or had your best interests at heart—he or she might add, "I think I will start to do just that, too." (Because that practice—that routine—is a good idea at any age!) And, well, why not? What are friends for, anyway?

What, you might wonder, has happened to common courtesy, too? Why do supposed friends and family seem so keen on pointing out these failings, or even notice them, as you enter that age, when they could be so much more supportive? Perhaps you might try to find the right time and place to suggest to them that their support would be welcome. Why should you have to struggle with this alone when the answers and resolution of these issues might be suggested by a thoughtful friend or family member? Regardless ... your main concern is how to handle these situations as easily as possible.

In short, if you have concerns about where you put things, just designate places—the most likely places, the places you have used most frequently in your life, the places you will look to—and then, choose as few as possible for each thing. As stated previously, use the same place for each particular thing, or the same place for a group of things—like a table near the door for all keys, a bag, or gloves—and be done with it! Let's move on ...

So you don't know why you came into this room in the first place?

(Forget, for the moment, about the fact that this has been happening to you for years.) Try this little technique and see what happens. Test this scenario: You come into the room and can't remember why. STOP! Turn right around, walk out of the room, and march directly back to where you were before, and wait. See how long it takes to remember! Yes, I bet you will remember! And it didn't even take you that long, did it? Especially if you don't block yourself by beating up on yourself and allowing frustration, anxiety, and embarrassment to enter into the picture. That's it!

When you get good at this and trust yourself, you may be surprised to find that you do not even have to walk back to the other room: You might simply be able to pause for a moment and "image" it (mentally return to the other room). Further, when you get really good at this (that means you acquire the confidence that this technique will work for you—and it will), you may just have to pause a moment, wherever you have gotten to, and lo and behold, you will remember why you came—or were going to come—into that room anyway!

So the question that could be asked, again, that would make sense for a friend or family member to suggest, that might be both kind and helpful, would be whether you found yourself going into a room and didn't remember why you were there. If your answer is "yes," then a tactful suggestion might be useful. Why should others have suggestions on how to solve this issue? Because this event happens to most people, at any stage of their life, and throughout their life. Some people have devised such methods to avoid this pitfall—so why not share the wealth? It's only information! One might wonder, again, why our friends and family are not more supportive?

I have not found one person who has never walked into a room and not known why he or she was there—not one! Usually, when I raise the question: "Do you ...?" a sheepish smile comes over the face of the person I am talking to almost immediately. So it appears to be the frequency of this happening, not the event, that is the problem here too—and since it ignores age, it seems to be truly a false indicia of losing it. Think about it! And talk about it!

Regarding the social scene: Kind friends and family have a basis for understanding, and if they wanted to be helpful, they could give some thought to how to deal with an excessive amount of this type of issue occurring—after all, it can get pretty annoying. Or if they were really concerned and cared about hurting your feelings, they might have done some basic research like "Googling" it. But if, for now, society is not being as supportive as you would like (in fact, you find social attitudes impeding you from building the life you want and can have), at this point, you will need to help yourself out of this dilemma by following suggestions like those described above. They really work!

Be that as it may: For those of you entering that age, three specific situations fraught with concern suddenly may no longer seem so formidable. Not that difficult to manage, really, are they? No real need to panic either, is there? As stated previously, there is no intent in this chapter and the next few to diminish the potency of these situations in which you find yourself. You are too astute not to know where these questions (including knowing looks, raised eyebrows, and the full panoply of devices used by people to indicate there is a serious problem here) are leading.

However, this chapter and others to come suggest there is a different way of looking at these so-called unalterable signs of aging: that there is both a different perspective and a different solution from the ones these friends and family members seem to be suggesting openly (or by their behavioral mannerisms) for many of the problem areas identified. My take on this is that these so-called indicia are based on patterns of sociological thought that simply, in large part, no longer apply to this age. If you still doubt it, pick up a current science or medical or university magazine and read the amazing work that is in progress to prolong a good life, to ratify that you are likely to have a wonderful future in store. So I must tell you that I truly believe the ongoing clinging to past attitudes and the behavior that flows from those outmoded social norms are beginning to sound a great deal like nonsense or, to use my favorite word: hogwash! Further, the questions being asked (including those looks and raised eyebrows) are misleading and insulting: You would do well to recognize them.

Recognizing the Question (Separating the Wheat from the Chaff)

An esteemed professor I will admire forever often told his students—of whom I had the good fortune to be one—to always check carefully whether the right question was being asked. I can still hear dear Mr. Sypher say, "But ... is it the right question?" Does what is being stated make sense? He repeated this often—it was one of his favorite refrains and teaching methods. Although a relatively easy method of critical analysis, it became an invaluable tool in life. Often, the questions or suggestions we were looking at were indeed wrong or misleading! Often, very wrong! They seemed applicable, maybe sensible, but on reflection, they really didn't or shouldn't have been applied to the issue. Now that you have perused through the three examples, I think you know that the wrong questions or suggestions are being raised. By these reactions, people seem to be asking directly or suggesting more frequently (or hinting with gestures or looks, equally unsettling, for they are implying that you are losing it in a rather strong manner) that you really ought not to be left on your own anymore. Be on the lookout for these suggestions or questions that lead to that conclusion. And be ready to respond appropriately.

One last look at how friends and family might be more helpful without trying too hard, instead of acting in the manner described throughout this chapter. You should be convinced, if you were not before, that many of these behavior patterns that perhaps cause you to be so self-conscious, so concerned—and yes, sometimes panicked about normal changes that come with the territory—are not really that devastating or that difficult to handle: They are simply the wrong suggestions, inferences, and questions! Further, people should know better—and if they took the time, they would know better. This is simply inappropriate behavior and, decidedly, the wrong attitude. Remember this, and remind yourself of it often. Further, friends and family should not be saying or hinting this at all: It is simply unkind, untrue, rude—downright unfriendly, wrong, and grossly misleading! Worst of all, these types of behavior patterns may interfere with the way in which you choose—or would like to choose!—to plan your life.

Concluding Remarks

Take a long moment and think about what has just transpired in the above three specific examples of responses to suggestions and questions that are being used to influence the Silver Generation's choice of lifestyle. Do you think you are incapable of putting the suggestions into effect? Of course not! In reality, they are not all that difficult to compensate for now, really, are they?

If you have been listening to the chatter around you that suggests you are rapidly moving to the end of the active life as you know it, you may already be packing your bags. However, if you have been paying attention, you already have begun to realize the utter nonsense the tendency is to attach such importance to such easy-to-address issues: simply a different approach, isn't it? And one that works! A rational, no-nonsense problem-solving technique works partially because you have done it all your life. No real difficulty here, once you think about it, is there? I think upon reflection and use of the simple changes in strategies and techniques suggested, many of you will agree.

Are you beginning to think that perhaps the societal norms that seem entrenched may well be, in great part, hogwash indeed, not applicable to the real world of the twenty-first century, not applicable to your world and your Silver Generation (if, indeed, they ever were)? I encourage you to put the simple steps identified in this chapter into immediate action and form your own conclusion. Once you have, I think you will take up the mantle and continue on in the spirit of compensating, tweaking, and learning a few new tricks to compensate for new issues that arise as you enter that age. It may be a bit challenging, but certainly nothing daunting that you cannot deal with once you put your mind to it. And if you have to work on it a bit … so what else is new?

As you continue to become more and more aware of your environment, awareness of the great divide will also become apparent, awareness that this society is not in sync with the needs of your dynamic new Silver Generation, awareness that it will be up to this generation—to you—to change the norms, not by convincing or arguing or debating, but rather by becoming aware that you have a right to question anew things that seem out of joint with the event. You have the right to reject those attitudes and behaviors that are not appropriate or tolerable; to proudly look for and utilize innovative solutions; to assert yourself. You have the ability, too, to debunk the myths that present hurdles to your full participation in a life in this world by living in this world—which is also your world—in the way you choose.

No, you will not be Don Quixote tilting at windmills: Science, medicine, and technology are fast changing the landscape of the way we look at the world, especially (and in particular) the world of those entering that age. And business, if not society, is starting to pick up the vibrations that life—your life, the life of your generation—might just last a long time: Look at this recent ad that appeared in a magazine, entitled "What will you be driving at age 119?" It states:

> *These days people are living to age 100 and beyond technology is helping them to live better. In the next few years, a major automobile company will introduce a car that can give you a check up while you are behind the wheel. It will be able to assess your stress level and adjust its performance, lighting and interior scent accordingly.*

After you have said, "Wow" or "I don't believe it," ask yourself why industry is suddenly turning up the volume and what it says about the Silver Generation. Give this ad a thought (look for others, too), and ask yourself why the business community is trying to attract the buyer of the future, no other than those entering that age who now may be expected to live past 100. In other words, this and other advertisements are starting to gear their products towards those of you who comprise the dynamic Silver Generation of this new century! Isn't this an indication that business is starting to look at you as a consumer, not as a drop-out of the system, gone to pasture? Nice to know, isn't it, that your world is beginning to regard you as a valued member? Mark my words: This century may turn out to be the Age of the Silver Generation. So when those questions and comments—and looks, too—are tossed at you, consider the question and suggestion; consider the source; and consider the not-too-difficult techniques to resolve them! Life—this life, your life— is certainly worth it!

Chapter 4

ABSENTMINDEDNESS AS A POSITIVE

An Original Theory

In this chapter, I present a very different view on absentmindedness: a positive look at this question quite different from what seems to be the prevailing social attitude. The following chapter changes the dynamics of those moments of absentmindedness to reveal a unique aspect of absentmindedness as a positive aspect of life, particularly when one has entered those silver years. In changing the landscape, I believe another myth of the aging process in terms of excessive concern by society on the effect of forgetfulness or absentmindedness may be at work here. So I explore this different focus for those entering that age to consider: Absentmindedness as a Positive!

Two things motivate me here: One of my favorite people, Albert Einstein, was reputed to be totally absentminded. I am doubtful whether anyone was brazen enough to point that out to him—and, of course, there were loving people around to attend to the more ordinary tasks of this beloved absentminded genius. Then there are the "absentminded professors" that we always used to refer to, who were always so busy thinking in their ivory towers, they simply couldn't be expected to pay attention to everyday things in the real world, like where they put things, or whether they walked out of a room when they meant to make themselves a cup of tea, or where in the world their keys were. Recognizable, pretty mundane stuff and far too distracting from their serious world of thought—we surely wouldn't want to interrupt them, and be responsible for interrupting a line of serious thought, now, would we?

Well, either we have a double standard (which we do!), or there is another explanation, which I much prefer: In certain situations, we accept absentmindedness as a positive. I posit here, that along with reaching that age and becoming forgetful, absentmindedness may merely be an indication of deep thought. Of course, if you think about it, haven't you been doing some of that all your life? Yes, you may be doing it with more frequency. (And yes, as suggested in the last chapter, it may be as a result of having entered that age.) Or maybe, more likely, because people seem to be scrutinizing your behavior more closely (and making a big deal over it), your absentminded moments are becoming more of a problem to you? Or perhaps you are thinking more deeply about many of the ideas that have been germinating in your mind for so many, many decades?

I suggest you consider that absentmindedness can be less a result of age and more a result of the knowledge acquired (the sum and substance of a lot of years of acquiring knowledge in that brain of yours), and the desire to consider multiple issues—more deeply—not because you have entered that age, but because you have acquired a treasure house of knowledge about which you prefer to think! Here is another example I recently came across: I have been reading a book where Elie Wiesel wrote this of his father: "He never knew; he was lost in his own thoughts. It took him months sometimes to notice that a person had entered our lives." Like Einstein's absentmindedness, the remark about Elie Wiesel's father was made with respect and admiration. So we see that absentmindedness can be viewed as a positive rather than a negative trait. Thus, with all respect, in this essay, absentmindedness is seen as a positive aspect of the thinking person—*especially those entering that age!*

I Am Thinking (*Cogito Ergo Sum*)

Now that I am past my sixties and have acquired so much longed-for knowledge, I am like my own vast encyclopedic resource: A person can reach such a stage of development, as we have seen in the life of Primo Levi, who taught a fellow inmate to speak Italian by teaching him Dante's *Inferno,* which was stored in his memory base, and another man who, while in exile, wrote an amazing piece of critical literature, drawing on the vast resources of his mind's library, since he had no access to books during this book-burning and people-in-hiding period. Thinking more about the notorious absentmindedness of the esteemed scientist, Albert Einstein, who, long before senility could come into play, was absentminded, and others similarly revered, I embrace this aspect of mental exploration.

Here is my theory in practice: I go about the house doing the chores of a lifetime, they are patterned in my head, I need not think too much about what I am doing. The tasks are automatic and routine. I am almost robotic as I go through my daily chores. On the other hand, what I am not robotic about—but I am almost, at times, maniacal about—are my thoughts. I seem to be always thinking! These, after all, are my silver years. This is a time for thought and reflection: on family, on future, on the big questions we humans seem to ask over and over again about life: What is it all about? What did it all mean? What does it mean? What have I done with my life? Did I do it all right or well? What am I doing now? What do I want to do? Can I do it? Do I have time?

For me, there are certain subject areas that I have toyed with for half a century, "played with," is the right term. No, they are not in my subject area of professional achievement: They are not in the subject of law, but life. Creation is one of the big areas: creation according to religion, according to myth and legend, according to science. The relationship between women and men is another: How did we get to the present hierarchy, division of labor, stereotypical characterizations? How did the tension arise and when? What was it like before recorded history? (That was not so long ago in the scheme of things.) What do the cave drawings and early sculptures and artifacts tell us, what was it like when Mother Earth ruled the world? Is there any doubt she did? How did humankind get so turned around anyway and never reach the conclusion from Genesis, where it says, "And God created man in his own image, in the image of God ... male and female created he them," that these words reflect an equality of male and females that we are just perhaps coming to fully embrace? All of these questions are connected in my mind to a degree and have always been; there is a puzzle there and the key to something larger than myself, if I can figure it out or start to—before ...

Mundane Chores and Tasks Are Lower on the Priority List

Well, my theory of absentmindedness is this: Whatever you are absorbed in, you are absorbed. You recognize that this will be your last opportunity to put it all together. You recognize that this will be your last opportunity to make any contribution, big or small, that you may hope to or want to leave for your family, friends, society, community, culture ... world, maybe. So you go about daily chores and routines without giving it a thought. And if you are lucky, nothing goes wrong. But if you are not really paying attention, if your mind is full, if you are thinking about your own things, then, if a routine thing goes wrong, if something is not in its place, if you put something where you don't usually put it, if you change one of the myriad habits and patterns you have established, WATCH OUT, you are lost—and feel befuddled.

So my theory is quite simple: Your mind is full of the things you have placed or had placed there by the vast educational process: grade school, high school, etc.; by your parents and others: id, ego, superego; and by contemplation of the current state of the world: politics, current events, and contemplation of the vast discoveries in science and medicine, not to mention the technical maze of the new great labyrinthian monster: the computer. AND YOU DO NOT THINK ABOUT MUNDANE DETAILS OF THE DAILY CHORES YOU ARE TRYING TO PERFORM. WATCH OUT! Sometimes— often?—you get into trouble. You are obviously not concentrating on the chore at hand.

Perhaps it is not your mind losing it, but more a function of your mind's overflowing and wanting to be heard. While my own theory about some of this seeming forgetfulness is not scientifically tested (to my knowledge), but rather the result of observation and experience, I believe it is plausible. Enough people seem to intuitively recognize the practice of it, many admit they indulge in it, and many others embrace it.

So once again, I say hogwash to the concept of absentmindedness as an indicia of senility and diminishing prowess of this Silver Generation slowing down, but rather as minds full and operative, on another level. Perhaps what this new and dynamic generation needs to do, rather than lament on some loss of mental function associated with age, is to learn to draw more fully upon its experience, knowledge base, and freedom as it enters that age. YES, there is more freedom to do as you please, more free time to engage a mind that may hold much richness and more freedom to think and expand upon your thoughts. In other words, for those entering that age, you may just have the time and freedom to relish that mind you have and explore its potential to the fullest.

If you need to reflect further upon this, you might want to go back and reflect on Einstein once again. You couldn't be in better company, now, could you? No one would dare accuse him of anything else BUT THINKING, LOST IN DEEP THOUGHT, now, would they? Or think of someone brilliant that you know or heard about—isn't one of her characteristics that her mind is always somewhere else? Or that he doesn't seem to concentrate on what is going on—that he is a dreamer?

The next time you find your mind wandering off, and before you fall for all the recent advertisements that feed into your fear—"Do you find your mind wandering? Do you find yourself in another world? We can help you stay in this one"—consider what you were concentrating on instead. You may just find what you were thinking about was far more worthwhile to you than continuing to concentrate on some everyday task—especially if you can set up a new routine to compensate for or avoid negative aspects of absentmindedness. You might find you can have your cake and eat it too—or that you can compensate for not paying attention to chores and tasks, and you can still continue on this path of most interest and satisfaction to you for the rest of your life.

Concluding Remarks

In this essay, I have presented a far different view of absentmindedness as a positive trait for your consideration. I categorically reject the attitude of absentmindedness as a negative and embrace absentmindedness as a positive aspect of life. Certainly, you will have to take steps to ensure that the necessities of life are attended to and that you don't become absentminded at the wrong time—but that is what the chapters on debunking myths are all about: ways to deal with, handle, compensate for, or cleverly take care of the ordinary chores and tasks of everyday life that must be done. Can you do it? Of course you can: You have not gotten this far in life without having an arsenal of tools, techniques, and strategies within your knowledge base, skill set, and abilities, now, have you? The more you put in practice and the more you set your routines, the more you free your time for thoughts and ideas of your liking and are able to shape the world to make room for the self you want to be.

So I ask, with all due respect: Is absentmindedness necessarily a scourge, or another of the raps our society seems to delight in pinning on those entering that age, the truth you can't avoid? Is the characteristic, so repugnant as to hide your head in shame, apologize profusely, and die of embarrassment, one more nail in the … Well, h— NO! I don't see it that way at all! What I see is a perfectly logical, sequential, chronological continuum of all the years you have had, all the splendid experiences you have lived, all the grand thoughts you have thought—in part or full; in other words, the fulfillment of all you are and all you hope to be! So I pause here to assert these thoughts on absentmindedness as a positive and hope you will call upon this theory as you walk through the portals as a member of the dynamic Silver Generation of the twenty-first century.

Chapter 5

DEBUNKING MORE MYTHS II

Questions That Should Not Be Asked!

What did you eat today? What day is it? What month? What year? What's new? The less subtle: What's going on in your life? **The downright rude**: What did you do today, yesterday, last week? Where did you go? What did you do? What did you call this? You can't think of his name? **The Responses: Marty/Cyrano/Boy Scout/ Girl Scout and Other Approaches.** When someone tests you by asking, "Who is the president of the United States?" look at him or her and say incredulously, "YOU DON'T KNOW? YOU BETTER SEE A DOCTOR!" (This is called Subtle Senility Testing Reversed.)

Moronic Questions For Senility Testing

As soon as the Silver Generation learns to exert itself with spunk and defiance where needed, a lot of the types of behavior found uncomfortable will stop. As soon as those entering that age no longer drop out of social settings, rapidly growing "grey power" will put an end to this type of nonsense. It is a holdover from another day that saw certain signs as evidence of diminishing capacity and, unfortunately, people taking advantage of it. I feel certain that these stereotypes of those entering that age will be put in their rightful place as were other moronic social mores that tried to determine the path of former generations. They will not, I believe, survive the new dynamic Silver Generation. Outdated attitudes and judgmental criteria must disappear. Members of this new, potentially dynamite generation will make their own paths.

When all is changing so rapidly for the better, with the possibilities for enhancement of living a very long and active life, and with potential use of your brainpower predicted for almost your entire life span, the old social norms that would embarrass and intimidate you—and leave you less than you are—have got to stop. Those entering that age have enough to contend with without answering to outmoded social norms that are not applicable to this day and age. Those of the Silver Generation must become aware, too, of these tests of senility and end them quickly. You do not need to be dealing with such nonsense. This chapter deals with some of those things that must disappear—and suggests multiple ways for you to choose how best to deal with what I call the moronic "testing for senility" questions that should not be asked.

First, Some Remarks

As an attorney, I have often thought how very awful it is to see older people subjected to certain questions as part of a determination of their competency. (Could it be because I have entered that age? Regardless, it makes me quite angry.) How dare anyone ask a question such as what day it is of a retired person, whose life is no longer tied to a day, a date, a time of year? Think about it: If the schedule is unchanged from Monday to Sunday, when no plans are different: no work; no coming home from somewhere; few scheduled appointments; no set time for breakfast, lunch, or dinner, except what a retired person arbitrarily sets for himself or herself, then why should one know? Why should or would a person in this situation even have the need to keep track of whether this is Monday or Tuesday—unless there is a specific appointment?

Ordinarily at this time of life, even if one continues working, he or she is no longer on clock time. The lifestyle has changed; the routines have changed. There is no car or train to take to or from the office, no people to speak to as a matter of course, no newspapers that those of us still on the fast track glance at or catch "news bites" on the way here or there that give vital statistics—day, date, season, event (often subliminally)—as they move around from place to place.

Why should a retired or semi-retired person be expected to know with impunity the day, the date, the month? These are the wrong questions! But the question is broader and has further implications: Why should any senior person, retired or semi-retired or absorbed in another venture or on another track, need to keep abreast of this unimportant data? To whom is it important, after all? Time is a mechanism of our industrial society, which runs on clock time: Anyone doubting this should take another look at Charlie Chaplin's classic *Modern Times.* Or remember the difficulty of early industrial efforts to put workers in Alaska on assembly lines and make them adhere to factory-fixed clock time. Yes, as you can imagine, they were initially a disaster in the land of the midnight sun, which sees six months of day and six months of night; people had adjusted differently to day, night, eat, work times—different biological clocks, no big surprise. I am fast becoming convinced that, in fact, lawyers should consider it an obligation to prepare an older client for those age-specific questions as they prepare others for court appearances. I hope they are listening.

Or another example, if one is living in Florida, California, Arizona, or any other place where the weather stays relatively the same, how is one to distinguish if the season is winter or summer or fall or spring? Those of us in New England have an advantage, of course: snow (must be winter); trees changing to red and orange (must be fall); to burnt orange and brown (must be end of fall); flowers (spring). A person can always make a conscious effort to keep abreast of these things, of course. Maybe one ought to, as a matter of routine, brush up for company (or when company is expected) to avoid those remarks and questions that are bound to come with their horrid implications and defining moments. It depends, of course, on whether they want to give a part of their time to something that means little in their everyday life anymore. It is just possible that retired and semi-retired people have other, more interesting, and to them, better things to do—like building a wooden horse, or refinishing or upholstering furniture, or painting that work of art, or writing that novel (or, well, any number of things that don't lend themselves readily to time starts and stops or seasonal changes in weather, for that matter). Does it really matter if they can't tell (or are not particularly interested in) what they had for dinner last night? It really doesn't matter much, does it? And it really doesn't prove anything either.

Or examine changing eating habits: First, it is a known fact that taste buds decline with age, and that as people age, they do not experience the gastronomical delights they once did when eating. Second, who is preparing the food and what are the choices, or are there even choices on a day-by-day basis, or does a person care? Do you care? Think about it? Why care when the three-times-a-day clock time is no longer operative in your life? Why care when you don't necessarily take those time-outs, or "breaks," as they are called in the business world, to eat breakfast, lunch, and dinner; have coffee; have a snack? Why our society and often our legal system put so much emphasis on whether or not a person remembers what they had for breakfast seems rather ridiculous when viewed in this manner, does it not? Or just plain mean and, at times, of impure motive.

I personally take issue with the questions discussed in this chapter. I consider these types of questions downright offensive and inappropriate.

I think, too, at my most cynical, that these unkind questions may, at times, be designed, in large part, to move the senior generation into another stratosphere, to remove them from competition, so to speak, to put them in a place where they can be easily handled with an assist from social institutions. I'm sure a case could be made for one or another of the variations of Freud's Oedipus/Electra complex here, and they may, indeed, have a bearing, but to me, Erik H. Erikson and his wife Joan M. Erikson were wiser. As they moved through the last stages of human development, they made this observation in *The Life Cycle Completed*:

> *We are tested on our "time identity" the normal societal model for old age has been to encourage letting go, but not to seek a new life and role—a new self. This promotion of false old age, or denial, stifles normal development.*

They had thoughts, too, about the "put-out-to-pasture" syndrome that society still appears bent on perpetuating. "Something is terribly wrong," the Eriksons stated, and they also asked this question: Why has it been necessary to send our elders out of this world into some facility so remote in order to live out their lives? Why indeed!

A Word on the Questions[5]

Questions meant to embarrass or catch you off guard; questions that shouldn't be asked but are; questions that are obvious senility

---

5   The questions presented here may seem to many sophisticated members of the Silver Generation out of the realm of possibility, probability, or interest: you are still active; you are still "with it" relatively, and so on ... but, at some point, you too will find you are at or have entered that age. I warn you: It can happen overnight, once you take yourself out of the marketplace for any reason whatsoever, including "working from home," or semi-retiring; these "moronic senility tests," as I designate them, will come into play! You may recognize these types of situations from earlier times, but you may not be prepared to have these social darts and arrows pointed at you. So you will want to be prepared, regardless of whether you feel it is not, or might never be, aimed at you.

tests (cleverly disguised, or so it is thought); which, if they catch you off guard can be embarrassing or leave you uncomfortable, are the focus of this chapter. This is a type of question (behavior patterns) that must be responded to promptly and definitely—with all the techniques you can muster. Fortunately, there are a multitude of techniques and strategies just waiting in the wings. Consider a few of these and you may just lessen some of the apprehension many feel in social situations. Maybe, too, you will find greener pastures rather than the ones you may now feel you are being led to, as too many of my friends report they are experiencing. You can learn to control situations that are bothersome to you—particularly as you enter that age—that somehow no longer seem witty, or smart, or wise (if they ever did), just rude and difficult, often downright uncomfortable, too. You can learn how to respond properly and live your life as you prefer to live it—instead of being concerned about questions others are asking that they should not be.

So with that in mind, we turn to a moronic set of questions that seem to be a holdover from another day, but are fraught with pitfalls for the unwary. Let's look then at what members of this Silver Generation face as we did in Debunking Myths in Part I, and how you might change the climate and turn things around when faced with the uncomfortable onslaught of the questions designed to imply you are at "that age" and there is "little hope." They are no more difficult to handle than the earlier ones: They are just dumber and more unkind. But make no mistake, these insipid questions, these moronic tests of senility, as I call them, need to be handled—rights must be asserted. If it seems that friends and family are just outside the door waiting to greet you with these "realizations," you can respond kindly, or you can get angry. Either way, members of the Silver Generation, you must fortify yourself with techniques to nip in the bud these implications and minimize or bury these questions that should not be asked.[6] You have too much at stake: These are deceptively simple questions; questions that may catch you off guard, leave you feeling you have entered a time of diminished capacity, and lead you into traps for the unwary.

I think you will find the techniques offered for your consideration both interesting and easy to master. Again, it is a matter of catching on to the game—but it can be a deadly game that can leave you feeling poorly about yourself, your ability to participate in the world around you, your real worth, and your confidence to handle life on your terms. Despite the seriousness of this section, you should have little or no difficulty adopting the techniques suggested: Marty, Cyrano, or the Girl Scout/Boy Scout motto: Be Prepared. Rather than the necessity to probe deeply into new arenas that require extensive skills or abilities, I think you will find merely the awareness of what is going on is all that is really necessary. These easy-to-absorb concepts can leave you feeling well prepared to meet the situations you may encounter. You can handle it! Remember: The goal is to enable you to take control.

---

6   To those readers who ask, what if they really want to make sure I am eating or getting enough sleep, and so on—questions of a well-meaning nature, that is, I would say, tell them to come over more often or go to lunch with you or talk to you more—or take you to a show or movie or watch the news with you and discuss things. Their real involvement and their real interest will readily give them the answers they need to have—but a "cross-examination" is not the proper method, and questions that are improper and inappropriate in the circumstances are not questions seeking real answers: some might call them trick questions aimed at eliciting already-decided-upon responses. Watch it! Test the motive. You are the one in charge, and you can change the rules at any time as long as you feel comfortable and in control.

The Questions & Responses: The Embarrassing and Intimidating Questions Amplified

Now, what did you eat today?

The Switch Technique

Many members of the Silver Generation have a great deal of success with a simple switch technique, because other people like to talk about themselves. So, in short, simply turn the question back without responding to it: "What did *you* have to eat today, dear?"—and then fire away: "What did you have? What are you having tonight? Are you going out? Where? What type of food do they serve? What is your favorite?"

Who can really argue with you or quibble that you don't remember what you ate that day? Maybe, by the time you are finished with these counter-questions, some of your friends and family will get the other point too: "This is annoying me!" And if you've had a chance to recover from the intent of the question—and we all get the intent—or you feel you must respond to their original question, try this: "My foods are fairly humdrum these days, not worthy of talking about," followed by: "Why don't we go out for lunch or dinner next week? You've got my salivary glands working." And you can always make the attempt to get to a worthwhile conversation: "I hardly notice what I have eaten, except to eat for nutrition." Ah … there's a great subject. "What do you think would make a balanced diet? What are the latest findings?"

What Did You Do Today?

Again, ask yourself: Is what is being asked the person's business? Do I want to discuss that? Give the polite response first (you're the nice gal or guy, remember), but then don't hesitate to use any or all of these techniques that seem comfortable for you. Or use any other skills you have mastered: annoyance, throwback, sarcasm, and downright irritation—you know the way. Try them out as often as you can: There is always the practice afforded and satisfaction from taking control of the situation.

The Throwback Strategy

This is related to the switch technique, but a bit more aggressive for those not getting the point: Would it be impolite to really take aim and throw back the question subtly (or not so subtly), such as: "And what did you do last Tuesday evening? Or last month? Or last year? Do you go to that restaurant we were at together in 1957? You remember— don't you? Oh, you don't? Tsk … Tsk …" (Get it?) "Where did we have that delicious soufflé? When was that exactly?"

Or if some supposed friend is really getting your goat: "Remember we bumped into ___ several years ago and she said ___; do you think that is still the case?" You might want to think a bit about this one, but you will relish the look on the face of a so-called acquaintance or friend or family member who is throwing these awful (and they are awful, and rude, too) questions at you.

Your so-called friends and family might just start to get the idea that you are not going to be a willing participant in these unkind, so-called social amenities. Perhaps, too, these social amenities are just holdovers from the times, part of the fabric of our social milieu, so to speak. However, I regard the term "amenities" as more of an excuse for bad behavior. Hopefully, these behavior patterns will disappear as other socialization attitudes and behaviors have, as I've repeatedly stated, but the stakes are simply too high for the Silver Generation to tolerate. So once again, this generation must be in the vanguard of change—in large part by responding in ways that let people know, in no uncertain terms where need be, this is no longer considered proper social conduct—even if it means aging defiantly (age, after all, has its opportunities and prerogatives). Remember: These are not games; they are a menace to your lifestyle—the one you prefer to live and will carve out for yourself even if it is with spunk, even if you need to be defiant.

The Marty Approach

"What do you feel like doing tonight, Marty?" (Or variations: "What's up? What's going on in your life? Where did you go? What did you do?" Or any type of question you regard as any variation of the "testing the acuity of your mind" approach.)

A potential response to the "What do you feel like doing tonight?" type of question is given by Marty (played by Ernest Borgnine) in the movie of the same name. I'm sure many of you also remember the simple, but eloquent, turning back of the question by Marty. "I don't know … What do *you* feel like doing?" Marty says with style—without missing a beat: laid back and firm. And so it goes! Marty and his "friend" go back and forth for a while: The same answer, but the refrain is always the same: simple, friendly, but very effective. How can anyone take real offense at that response?

That would be my suggestion: Don't give an answer. Let the questioner be sorry he or she asked. Practice asserting yourself. It's easier to learn to utilize these techniques for keeping others off your back if you use the ones that are easiest or come most naturally and then go on to the others that may demand more practice. Again, take it as you like it.

A variation of the Marty approach is this, what I call the open-ended questions people seem to thrive on asking—especially as it is seems to come up a lot. To the insipid, open-ended question: "What's up?" consider the simple, but highly effective: "I don't know, what's up with you?" And come to a dead stop! Why not just answer the question? That, of course, is an option; except, after you have answered as fully as you'd like, the next question can invariably be another stinger: "What else?" Or a value judgment: "That's all?" Or "That doesn't sound too exciting." As with all things, you decide, based on the circumstances, what response you want to make. Marty makes a similar response to his mother when she asks, "What are you gonna do tonight, Marty?" His response … you got it: "I don't know, Ma."

Here's another example from a master of a different approach, but an equally effective one:

The Cyrano Approach

You might like this Cyrano approach—at the other end of the Marty approach. As many of you know, this is one where the questioner or person who made the meant-to-be-snide, demeaning, and insulting remark is sorry he or she ever made any remarks by the time Cyrano completes his response. (Cyrano is the hero is Edmond Rostand's play *Cyrano de Bergerac*.)

When someone tries to insult Cyrano by making an unseemly remark about his long nose, Cyrano kind of huffs nonchalantly, and in effect replies, "You call that an insult? If you were going to insult me, you might have said …" and then he goes on to give twenty examples of better insults the person could have used to really make the point: humorously, sarcastically, boldly, slyly, and so on. How wonderful for you to have twenty different ways to respond to those who attempt to put you down. In the end, he has totally embarrassed and humiliated the would-be maker of insults.

Here's how this technique can work for some of the moronic tests for senility discussed here.

Question: "What are your plans (or what have you done) this week? Last week? Last month?"

Response: "Now where shall I start?" And with this, a Cyrano response would be perfect: Go into a monologue, of course. (I would suggest no less than five minutes in duration and make it as long, boring, and drawn out as you wish; or as interesting as you like.) Or change the turf and say, "I'd rather discuss my plans for next week." And go on into a similar monologue. Or you can say, "I'd rather discuss what I might like to do" (which, as you get good at this, will give you a lot of maneuvering possibilities, but I'll leave that one to you).

If Cyrano can give twenty ways of describing a nose, you can find a number of fun ways of describing what you did, didn't do, or might do. You might want to practice for this one—after all, you want it to be as smooth a presentation as you can manage: It takes a bit of preparation, but it is well worth it (and it may well give you a certain degree of confidence).

You might want to start by filling in the above examples when you have a few minutes and thinking about how you might present them. It goes under the heading of preparedness—and besides, it will give you ready responses to dumb questions. You might even find some fun in provoking and chiding your would-be perpetrator. (At some point, you might want to retreat to a subject you know well and like to talk about—and maybe haven't gotten the chance to—and deliver a monologue on that.) Surely, you will be provided with the opportunity to use whatever you have prepared.

Questions and subjects—often ludicrous—thrown at you to test your ability to fully participate in social affairs deserve these monologue-type responses. I would urge you to look at the real Cyrano's remarks (Act I, Scene IV). One last word on Cyrano's artful response to the inadequate insult to his nose by putting forth any number of responses you would be pleased with yourself for making. We can't all hope to be Cyrano, but there are wonderful pointers from this wonderful monologue that can be extremely instructive: You won't be disappointed. The gift he has left for all time is a suggestion of multiple ways in how your response can be stated effectively. In short, with a little bit of practice, you can say exactly what you want to!

What tone do you want to use? It depends on your mood, and the way in which the unwelcome question or remark is made, doesn't it? So do you want to be aggressive, friendly, deceptive, curious, gracious, truculent, solicitous, thoughtful, pedantic, flippant, grandiloquent, dramatic, admiring, lyrical, naïve, respectful, rustic, military, practical, or parody—surely you can find one of these tones, á la Cyrano, to suit your taste. I suggest, if you have a few minutes, go see the play and read (or reread) that pertinent part of *Cyrano de Bergerac*. (You will also find some Cyrano-type responses in Chapter 13, on Intimidation Management.) You may feel extremely fortified getting a few responses under your belt á la Cyrano.

I'm sure you will find these suggested responses equally good for the many situations you meet. For those theatrical ones among you, those with a dramatic flare, this is sure to be a winner: Practice a monologue or two—as suggested above; retreat to a subject you know well, and see if anyone even interrupts you. I think you will find no one will. You might even be rewarded. And you will make your point.

The Girl Scout/Boy Scout Motto Technique: Be Prepared

Knowing people are coming (or you are going out), why not simply get a paper, turn on the radio, or have the "idiot box" (TV) turned on to a news station that will give you all sorts of good information: day, date, time of year; who killed whom; what trial is going, or go online? With a little practice, you can become a quick study of nonsense info that is very current indeed; in fact, so current, your visitors may not yet have heard about the latest news. Depending on what you are in the mood for, you can listen to the "tabloid-type" news stations, if your company likes gossipy non-news stories, or you can turn on the serious news stations: PBS ("The News Hour with Jim Lehrer") or CSPAN 1, 2, or 3, where you can pick up direct hearings from the Senate and House sessions. Bloomberg (finance and stock market news) is another good source, as are the National Public Radio (NPR) stations in your area—a good source of news—or catch the highlights on your computer Web page and go to the stories of your choice. This will definitely give you confidence. Just give them a Cyrano monologue of the day's events—and don't let them interrupt. That ought to hold them for at least a week, maybe more.

My dad used to call me at 7:00 in the morning; he knew I'd be up and that I wouldn't have left for work yet. He'd rattle off the most seemingly arcane things; he'd tell me things that were going on in the world that I thought were not possible. I'd get off the phone and, forgive me, wonder for a moment if he were losing it—until, one day, the trains were late and overcrowded, and I had the rare chance to read more than page one of *The New York Times* on my way to work. Was my face red: My father, in his late seventies, and retired, had simply read the paper from cover to cover. A great lesson for me; a great awakening too. I loved it! I also never again questioned the power of his mind or his intelligence!

So the point here is to be on top of it: Be like the Boy Scouts and Girl Scouts: BE PREPARED! A little preparation goes a long way to ward off the nonsense—and there is a lot of nonsense out there. Be convinced people have no right to invade your personhood; they have no right to jump to conclusions; they have no right to intimidate, embarrass, make you falter. Do not succumb! Remember that maxim: The best defense is a good offense. Meet the challenge! Greet it! Defeat it—and you'll get rid of some of life's most annoying, vexing, boring, and insignificant social areas that may nonetheless be putting a damper on what could be a very rich and creative part of your life. Don't let that be taken from you.

So When People Ask Those Questions They Shouldn't

There are no hard and fast rules here ... these suggestions are offered to give a start to a more positive approach to how to get out of the awkward situations those of the Silver Generation invariably find themselves in, and to take control when people ask those questions they shouldn't. Always, the object is to see the situation more clearly, be less uncomfortable (or intimidated), change the subject where necessary, and take control. The suggested responses can get you out of uncomfortable social dilemmas. The goal: to have your life be what YOU want it to be. You steer your course, and sometimes, knowing you have that right, you have the capability to do it—and just getting that control will set you on a new course: yours! With a little practice and some levity, you will get the hang of it quickly and be off and running, using your own creative brain bank.

As I'm sure many of you have noticed, often the questions being asked to determine your ability to continue a productive life are the wrong questions. Again, I would call most of these indicia hogwash, and I hope, by this juncture, you have begun to agree. The most important thing here is what you think of yourself, not what others think; that they tend to fit you into a stereotype is their problem; they have not caught up with this new generation. You are leading it! Don't forget that salient point: What happens, how you reach it, and how you allow others to affect your life is your decision.

Some of these embarrassing and possibly intimidating questions that should not be asked are controllable, some of them are avoidable, some of them are unconscionable—and some don't really matter much. Sometimes, you must develop defenses to take control of your life. It is your life, after all. Are you ready for the challenge? Are you ready to lead your own life? I think so! Are you ready to put aside outdated, outworn theories of behavior patterns and respond appropriately? You should be, especially if these questions create for you an environment that is not conducive to being the "you" you want to be. You will have to make the choice.

The social situations that are dealt with in this chapter are almost always directed to those entering that age. They set up false criteria to judge you. They are often cruel and inconsiderate. They often take place where you least expect them—in a wide universe: in the home, on a visit, out to lunch, on the phone, and other social environments. They are said by some to simply be non-thoughtful social amenities that are habitual—not meant to be hurtful. However, I regard them differently: I regard them as ugly, crude, rude, deliberately hurtful—sometimes vicious. They seek, intentionally or otherwise, to put a stigma or label on the person they are directed towards, and they are almost always directed to a member of the Silver Generation. More often than not, there is the concomitant implication that the person the remark is addressed to is losing it. Often, these so-called "social situations," meant to be sources of enjoyment, have just the opposite effect on members of the Silver Generation than they have a right to expect. They leave many exhausted, uncomfortable, and, even sometimes, lead to the unfortunate questioning of their own ability to live independent and productive lives.

Obviously, too much is at stake to leave this kind of social activity uncontested. There is too much, too, that comfortable social environments can afford, especially for those entering that age —and as you go through this book, you will see how they can be vehicles for sharing treasures that you have yet to explore and thoughts you have yet to share.

Concluding Remarks

To those of the Silver Generation with a high regard for themselves, and a strong desire to live their lives as fully as possible, social behaviors described in this section become totally unacceptable! Social environments that allow members of the Silver Generation to continue to participate, communicate, and give as well as gain enrichment will benefit all. In the last analysis, what members of this new dynamic generation want from social environments is nothing more, really, than an environment where good manners, consideration, and respect for all its members is the norm: Very worthwhile values, don't you think? Not earth-shattering. Oftentimes, reminding people of the expected behavior patterns will serve as the only needed reminder. After all, good manners, courtesy, and consideration have really not gone out of style. All will gain from the results of a more embracing and considerate social milieu.

But if it takes spunk and defiance to carve out a more hospitable social environment than you currently have; if it takes standing up for what you have a right to expect; if it takes effort and thought to ensure that you are afforded the social settings you will need as part of the fulfillment of your life; so be it! It is well worth doing! After all, this is your world as well. But for now, this new Silver Generation must learn to handle these hurdles in order to live and maintain a rich, full, and generous life—which is what this generation seeks, demands, and will have. No longer part of the "put out to pasture" mentality, your generation will do what it needs to do: You have the capacity, the skill, the motivation—and whatever else it takes to make your own way. If, in part, that means you show the spunk and defiance to insist that people in the social settings you choose to be a part of do not act in ways that are insulting to your intelligence and abilities to participate, so be it. Changes can be dealt with! Your world is too large, your life is too long, and your health is predicted to be magically too good (both mind and body) to allow obstacles and hurdles to be put in your way, deliberately or otherwise.

With a generation moving into a new century that promises health, longevity, and the ability to remain active both physically and mentally, the social situations that perpetuate these negative and demeaning behavior patterns—the implications of which are quite clear—must be stopped. At this point, as with so much else, it falls to those entering that age to actively change this social environment so detrimental to them. Why is it worth it? Because you have the right to "live the life you have imagined," as Thoreau reminds us, and if, in order to do that, you must "be the change you wish to see in the world," as Gandhi inspires, you are in good company.

Chapter 6

TURN ON THAT HUMOR SWITCH

Humor is man's greatest blessing.
—Mark Twain

Entering that age has its moments! No argument on that! How much more smoothly the path can be made with humor and levity. Those who march through life that way already know that; those who don't should consider taking a moment and making humor a factor in their lives. Not all of those entering that age can make the Comedy Show, but courting humor can be a tremendous help in attaining your goals: Yes, you have a lot on your plate; yes, it is an important time in your life, but it is also an extraordinary one if you have been paying attention to what this amazing century is bringing you and the gifts it will continue to lavish upon you. So, as the beloved Al Jolson once sang out, "Smile and the world smiles with you; cry and you cry alone." Well, we can't all be Al Jolsons but we can make the effort to lighten up a little bit—remind yourself every day what this world may hold in store for you—and you can SMILE!

A Positive Mind-Set

Many years ago, Norman Vincent Peale wrote the best-selling smash hit, *The Power of Positive Thinking*. That wonderful little book made its way throughout the land and into the hands of many of us;

somewhere my tattered copy lies around. Perhaps you have one too? I think many of you may remember the concept very well; it made sense. It told us to look for the silver lining, look on the bright side, find something good rather than something bad in things, think positively rather than negatively, see the glass as half full instead of half empty … and above all, remember to look at things with humor and levity.

Mind-set forms the basis of so much in our lives; the right mind-set or perspective can take you far; the wrong one—well, it doesn't seem to get you very far, to say the least. We all know people who are always complaining—nothing seems right; no matter how many things go right, they focus on the one thing that is wrong.

We all do this to a certain extent, but the fact that the nomenclature of Peale's book has become part of our general store of knowledge means we like people better who look at things in a positive manner, and vice versa, and we like ourselves better—we actually feel better when we think positively (substitute: are in a good mood). We would like to emulate that good outlook; nevertheless, we also know we often need to be reminded to maintain a positive attitude. Yes, it takes time and it takes practice. How do we push aside the negative attitude habit of a lifetime: the complaining and the worry; the seeing the worst of things; the readiness to embrace what is wrong rather than what is right? The enormous number of copies of that little book that were sold, *The Power of Positive Thinking,* tells us there were and are many people who wanted to seek this higher ground and that given all the concerns in our world today, there are probably many who would benefit from a more positive attitude.

But I have been talking about the more personal activities of everyday life. How many things on an everyday basis annoy you? We want everything to go well. Why can't it? Why can't people you expect to do things, do them? Why are you left waiting in offices, or left holding on the phone? Why don't people show up when they say they will? Why did the light turn red just before I went through it? Why is there all this traffic? Why is it raining? Recognize yourself?

All of this drains you, annoys you … leaves you feeling down: make a list of your own. Do you think for a moment that the person who cut you off feels bad (if the driver even noticed)? Do you think you can change the way the light changes in front of you? (Maybe, if you have a smart light—and know exactly where to stop your car.) Think: How important, really, are the 101 little bits of things that you allow to annoy you? And how important is it to your general health and well-being, as well as to your attitude, the way you face each day for you to let these things go? Well, science and medicine are reporting it makes a difference; it can make a large difference even perhaps to how quickly you get well, how you feel overall—and this is just the beginning.

Instead of the draining negative attitude about everyday annoyances, you might just try to be positive about the possibilities, the potential, the opportunity of every single day. I can think of nothing that has as much immediate gain in your life as the adoption of a positive attitude, looking at things positively, and smiling more often. If you can see your way through to this more positive outlook, I think it will add something of value to your life to further the goals, plans, and dreams you have as you enter that age, which many already see as the Age of the Silver Generation.

I know of two wonderful personal examples of how I believe a positive mind-set can make a difference. A couple I know well has this sunny personality between them. They have this gift of being witty and funny, and twisting and turning a phrase so that it brings smiles and laughter. They know they have this gift, and they practice it with each other: Their ears listen for the opportunities; their eyes show the glimmer of mischievousness as they realize that a phrase has a double entendre or lends itself to a funny remark or a pun; they are quite good at it and quick. To see them turn to each other even before the gem is unfolded, the laugh and smile beginning to appear, is to delight in the fun and frivolity and cleverness of that moment. Fortunate to be in their company for a decade, my spouse and I basked in this joy and brightness. Suddenly bereft of their company, we are the lesser for it; my mate and I are not similarly made; writing this has suggested that we lighten up and put some of that lighter touch in the way we look at our world.

It will take practice, we know, but it is worth the effort, especially because we know from our medical and scientific information that laughter and fun are indeed part of a healthier outlook and healthier body, which we are all striving for. Yes, one can change habits of a lifetime: It takes effort, but it can be done! Our fun friends are not without serious problems and serious concerns about all the things we are, they just know the joy of living— must include time for a good joke.

The other friend's role model comes out of physical problems and difficulty. A funny, successful man with a gift for story-telling and pulling your leg, he is in his second decade of Parkinson's disease. Not to be stopped, he makes and succeeds in an effort to remain positive, on top of things, interesting—and yes, funny. I'm sure that it is not without enormous effort and that he has his bad moments, but there he is ... he will not let this disease spoil his fun and personality. A truly inspiring model. If he can hope and travel and not disrupt his lifestyle ... then a positive attitude towards dealing with the silliness and stifling effect of social mores that have not caught up with the science and medicine should not be that difficult, now should it?—especially since it affords this Silver Generation such positive outcomes as a reward.

So whether you take out your tattered copy of *The Power of Positive Thinking* or just remember what its message is and try to incorporate it into your life once again, the second time around may just be easier. One further note: When someone smiles at you when you are walking along a street (except in big cities), doesn't it make you feel a bit uplifted? When you smile at someone, a passerby, or even someone who holds open the door for you, doesn't that put you in a different frame of mind? Maybe you smile back and say, "Thank you," or if it is a comfortable place, maybe you even utter, "Have a nice day!" How does it make you feel? Take note.

I leave you with this image: I came from New York; I never smiled at people who passed me on the street. Only a few hundred miles north, I found a different climate: People actually smile, people say hello, people ask, "How are you doing?" And no, they don't generally want to go beyond that pleasantry. So I have joined in the local tradition and am definitely the better for it. This part of the world does get cold sometimes, too—very cold: We have had severe snowstorms in the past that brought frigid weather—at least to my way of thinking. To survive, I dressed in fur; not politically correct now, but it was then. I have a big fur coat and a big fur hat that covers me almost entirely: People smiled when I went by. Inevitably, they smiled and made a pleasant remark. I smiled back—I know the smiles gave me a good feeling. I don't wear fur anymore ... but I am seriously thinking I will get out that old coat: Maybe I can get those smiles again.

Consider coupling these experiences with two new concepts that have been floating around from my own personal experience—gifts given to me by others—that I have found enormously helpful. "Don't beat up on yourself" (that's not what life is about) and "Every day is the first day of the rest of your life." I'm sure you have heard both of these before, but recently I have found both these concepts work wonders for my disposition. You may have to get to work modifying those old behavior patterns—but it is possible to do so, and the rewards are so many: brighter, lighter, happier days. Think about it: Isn't it worth the effort? By now, you know it is—and as my younger son has said to me at various points in my life, "No pain, no gain," so think of your goal: no less than charting a course that includes a smile and a positive attitude. It can make a difference for the rest of your life. Here are two examples of the concepts.

Don't Beat Up On Yourself

On the other side of the warm, wonderful people who, with their bright smiles, light up their faces and the world, are those whose habits take them to Dumpsville, U.S.A. They beat up on themselves (the vernacular perhaps for self-flagellation). I mean no criticism; one is probably born with a predisposition (i,e., a gene), but by this time in your life you also might have noticed that environment (both people and place) and willpower also have important roles to play in personality and can have a significant impact on lives. By this time, too, you undoubtedly also know some things definitely make you happier, some things make you feel the other way. If you are smart, you seek out those better moments, as well as seek out people who bring a smile to your face and make you laugh. Sometimes, too, you get lucky—and sometimes, if you are open to new experiences, you learn from others.

A few years back, I tried biofeedback to assist in the easing of migraines, which were interfering with my life in a way that was rendering me somewhat dysfunctional—like a robot moving through my days. I was lucky to find a biofeedback doctor whose background in psychology and psychotherapy turned out to be helpful. In a small but comfortable office, she created a restful and trusting environment. Together, we diligently went through the mechanics of relaxation techniques, of de-stressing, of breathing exercises. While connected to a machine, I would see the bright red light of high stress (with which I usually entered these sessions) slowly turn green as I began to understand the strength of relaxation techniques, both physically and mentally.

When I arrived, she always asked about my day, and I would reiterate the stress events of the day, or when I came with a serious migraine, what events led up to it, including nutrition. I worked diligently and seriously with her: I was discovering many things about my day, my attitudes, the foods that were migraine triggers—and when I left, the migraines had receded (they were not gone, but minimized). The small change was enough to allow me to hope that I could, indeed, get some control over this monster that had distressed me for so long. (Those of you out there who have suffered with migraines will quickly understand; the other lucky people will just have to imagine a pain that grows and grows over hours and days and finally, when it lifts, you know it will return again too soon and without warning—and totally interfere with your life.)

One day, I came in and when she asked me about my day, I began by saying how stupid I had been (I ate the wrong food, when I should have known better; allowed myself not to get sufficient sleep for a few nights straight, etc.). When she could not deal with the way I was blaming myself, castigating myself, she said, "STOP! That is not what this is all about—not at all!" She was speaking of self-flagellation and mind-set. I was stunned that this gentle, low-profile, calming influence on my life should suddenly raise her voice: not high, not loud—but enough. I never forgot her lesson: Don't beat up on yourself! To this day, that bit of advice is there for me. And yes, I forget ... but then, after a while, I remember her lesson and thank this understanding person for this truly valuable gift.

Every Day Is the First Day of the Rest of Your Life

The other lesson on the benefit of a positive mental attitude I owe to a young man at a gym I go to. Always there to greet, always happy to see me (and everyone else, I suspect), he nonetheless greets me pleasantly. When it has been so long in between visits, and I am somewhat embarrassed by the interval that has passed—and I am badgering myself with promises I have made and not kept—this young man finds the right thing to say to me. In response to my lame excuses: "I just haven't been able to—I feel so bad," he (like my biofeedback doctor) stops me short with a smile and says, "But you're here now!" Often, too, he adds, "Remember, this is the first day of the rest of your life!" Maybe it is the tone of his voice. After all, I know this is one of those clichés—but, cliché or not, he seems to really mean it. And I am better for his saying it! It always makes me feel good! Always—because I do believe he means it! And at that moment, I see the fuller side of life instead of the other. These two short little helpful hints strangely enough give me pep talks when I have needed them and put me on the course of positive thinking when I need reminding (which seems to be less and less often).

Concluding Remarks

It is reported medically that people with a positive attitude heal better, can get through problems easier, and on an everyday basis, are apt to feel better and be happier. Remember this as you go through your day and the small annoyances start to pile up: You control your world and your time. Wherever you are, whatever room in the house; whatever place outside—you decide whether to go or not, whether to stop or stay, whether to look out one window or another. Remember, too, that you are the center of your universe. Which window will you choose to look out on the world, your world? You decide. Take control!

Practicing this art—and it does take practice—should enable you to feel better to live your life as you want to live it as you age with dignity, integrity, and spunk—and yes, defiance. It can give you that extra edge; the difference between failure and success is sometimes only your attitude. Remember the line, "Success is failure turned inside out, the silver tint to the clouds of doubt"—keep it in mind.

And if you are one of the lucky ones who already are inclined to be in the positive mode—and I'm sure there are some out there—do the rest of us a favor: Your liveliness, loveliness, and positive energy are needed by those you come in contact with. Share your gift. So find your way to that mind-set that affords you a better way to live your life in a way that pleases you, that allows you to be the self you want to be, that allows you to go through the silver years positively.

So dust away that negative attitude and remember: This is the first day ... and if you forget, remind yourself, and if you lose it once in a while, don't beat up on yourself—at least not too often. Do something to get yourself back on track: take a long walk along a river, see the beauty of the flowers in spring, the leaves in fall, the snow on the trees in winter—whatever makes you feel good. Go to a concert or get a radio and listen to music you love; treat yourself to earphones; take a day and do nothing: vegetate; or if you do that too much, have lunch or dinner with a good friend, someone easy and relaxing to be with; take in a good movie or sporting event. You know what you like; you haven't gotten this far without knowing what really pleases you and makes you feel good. Do it! (If you don't really know, don't you think there is no better time to find out, to experiment, to start?) Make a list and act on it. Above all, get on with your life with the best mind-set and most positive outlook you can muster, and remember, always remember to smile. You will be greatly rewarded.

> *Humor is a great thing, the saving thing, the minute it crops up, all our hardnesses yield, all our irritations and resentments slip away and a sunny spirit takes their place.*
>
> *—Mark Twain*

Chapter 7

DEBUNKING MORE MYTHS III

What do you do when you encounter those dreadful moments and can't find a word or lose a train of thought? These issues appear to be among the more unsettling situations faced by members of the Silver Generation: They are widely talked and hinted about—and have all my friends (and myself as well) looking for the signs under every bush; the innuendoes that appear to go with this, too, strike deep into the hearts of those entering that age … But they are manageable: You have not come all this way in your life without the ability to handle these vicissitudes of life, now, have you?

Why Can't I Remember That Word? It Used to Be So Easy? What Happened to That Train of Thought? I Seem to Lose It So Often?

What do you do when you encounter those dreadful moments and can't find a word or retain your train of thought? These issues appear to be among the more unsettling stigma used to negatively characterize members of the Silver Generation. They are widely talked about and hinted at—and have all my friends (and myself as well) looking for the signs under every bush: The innuendoes that appear to go with this strike deep into the hearts of those entering that age. It is the sudden forgetting of a word or the not-readily finding of a word that you want to use; it is the losing of a train of thought as you look around and yes—admittedly—start to panic. Recognize the situation? You can't help but wonder, "Where am I?" No denying it is acutely discomforting and highly deceptive because once panic sets in, the discomfort, the apprehension, the worry, and the concern provide the very environment in which the feeling you are losing it is likely to rear its ugly head.

As in preceding chapters, two things should be considered: Haven't you always lost a word or train of thought? Did you ascribe it to loss of memory? Or loss of thought process? Or brain degeneration of significant consequence? Of course not! So now, somehow, why has it become (as it has for so many of the Silver Generation) one of the definitive signs, I think many readers will identify with, of catastrophe on the horizon for which you are incessantly on the lookout? You are ultra-concerned you will not find that word; you listen—so much more closely—to yourself; you stiffen or tense up; you may even, at times, get sweaty. You wonder: Will anyone notice? Has anyone noticed? Are they treating me differently? What can I do? Is all lost? Well, you know the routine. Why all the hyper-scrutiny? How much of the issue of a loss of word or train of thought is disintegration, and how much panic? Hard to say!

But isn't it commonly known that when you get tight and stressed, you tend to freeze and the smooth flow of words and thoughts becomes harder to convey? I would venture a guess that most of you have had this experience sometime or another. I think it fair to suggest, too, that perhaps, at times, you have become your own worst enemy. Aren't you allowing your fears and excessive concern to put you in the very position where the word is less likely to come? And if it doesn't appear quickly, aren't you also more likely to lose your train of thought as well—double whammy, self-induced, self-fulfilling prophecy? Think about it!

The previous chapters have suggested that this Silver Generation can easily deal with many so-called signs of aging that are often mistakenly used as false indicia of deterioration and loss that must lead to abandoning independent living. In fact, those concerns are wrong—and these are wrong as well: They are just two more issues that, once better understood, can be managed. While the problems discussed may be signs of normal wear and tear, and may be annoying, they can be dealt with! In Debunking Myths and Debunking More Myths II, the issues discussed are seen to be compensable with minimal effort—not rocket science—and I imagine few readers will think they are. (And some readers may, in fact, be rocket scientists—no one being immune from entering that age.)

In this further chapter on debunking more myths, the questions raised may seem more daunting, but by now, you should begin to suspect that the concern is largely unfounded. Once again, these attitudes and behavior patterns are simply wrong—what else is new? If you are beginning to understand what I have said up to this point, you will feel ready to debunk the next few myths presented: You already have all the skills you need.

Myth, as I have used the word, is not as much finding societal attitudes and the consequent behavior patterns of others toward the Silver Generation as totally untrue, but rather the heavy-handed way it is presented and accepted as if it were an absolute and, therefore, as if nothing can be done about it, and further, as if it must lead inevitably to a radical change in life pattern (because it will mean you have lost it).[7] The myth, here, is not the fact that you may well face these issues as you enter that age, you will; or face them more frequently, you will; the myth is that you will not be able to do anything about it—to compensate, to learn new skills, to change your behavior patterns, to handle it. You can! That is the myth, and it is a potent one. Hopefully, you have a clearer sense of what is happening and are becoming convinced that there are ways around these issues: ways to avoid them, ways to compensate for the loss, ways of handling them. Acceptance of this social attitude is not an option. At a minimum, it may result in a grin-and-bear-it demeanor, or at the point it happens, perhaps a wince—maybe only noticeable to you—but in either case, not pleasant. Again, haven't you bought into an attitude that says, "See, you have entered that age; you are losing it; it is inevitable and irreversible—and life, as you know it, is over"? WELL, IT IS NOT!

Don't buy into that! There is absolutely no need to do so. Even if you have noticed changes from previous behavior patterns, even if you have convinced yourself—which you shouldn't—that cells die with aging and they are irreplaceable, you know what to do now. Ask the questions: Is it true? At what point does it happen? Can I compensate? Is it an irretrievable loss? What do the scientific studies show? Again, if you have been paying attention, you know it is time to examine these situations more closely because 1) they may not be true, and, if true,

---

7   "Losing it" is one of those nefarious phrases that stand as a short cut to those in the know that a person is losing the ability to function as they previously did, and along with it, "and you know what that means," and the raised eyebrow, that indicates—again, to those in the know—that the person (you!) needs to be carefully watched and monitored for other signs of debilitation that will surely confirm that the time has come for them to be put out to pasture. In other words, it is a short cut by which gross generalizations, often wrong, are applied to those entering that age, which somehow makes the person doing this awesome critical analysis seem important: an ego trip at your expense; most often "full of sound and fury, signifying nothing"! Remember that.

you can most probably do something about the change in behavior, just as you hopefully are doing with the issues discussed in earlier chapters, and 2) these issues may simply be another perpetration of a hoax—maybe by friends and family who are well-intentioned, but out of sync with current research and, certainly, with the way in which you want to conduct your life.

Science is sending signals that these natural behavior patterns in older people—word difficulties and losing a train of thought—may be temporary failures, "tip of the tongue" phenomenon for loss of a word as well as other reasons for loss of a train of thought, but that they should cause no real concern. Studies are suggesting that things other than lessening or loss of mental faculties can be playing a part in these lapses, like medication or disease or nutrition or physical problems, many of which are reversible, and many more which will be handled better in the future—your future! These other factors should be considered first by those entering this age—before allowing panic to set in.

Other reasons are possible too: Maybe a word is taking longer to reach you—after all, you do have a great deal of knowledge, information, experience, and other things stored within your memory banks; did you ever consider that? You should! Or maybe you have more to search through, more to sort and sift through? Or maybe you have just come to a mature point in your life where you search for the exact word to express your meaning best and that sometimes, it backfires a bit? It seems the reason is not really known with certainty—and at this point in your life, does it really make a difference as long as you can compensate, handle, and control the situation? I don't think so.

By this time, too, you are beginning to realize that a distinction should be made between the natural loss associated with aging and the loss of ability to live and participate fully in life. It takes so little effort to compensate for potentially leaving boiling water on a stove, or not being able to find your keys, or going into a room and not remembering why you are there. The compensation strategies presented in previous chapters are not that difficult to put into effect. (You have all the tools you need—and if you have tried them, you know they work!) So it is with these "high-on-the-list-of-concern" issues presented here! You should know that the "inevitability" part may just be more nonsense, and you should have a healthy skepticism about the correctness regarding societal attitudes related to these issues for your generation: They are wrong! Not true! Needn't happen!

If you have understood that your generation is at the beginning of a new age and that you will be the leaders and the pathfinders, you will be more ready and willing to take charge, to join with others in your group to clear a path for the adventures and fulfillment that wait for you in this promising new century, especially for those members who take control of life. I also believe that once you get the knack of how to handle these issues, you will need little tutoring. I believe the solutions will come very naturally. The main need, as I see it, is to make you aware of the techniques for these situations, and many of you will be able to successfully take it from there.

Let's examine these issues more closely then…

As with the examples given in the previous chapter, there are some easy techniques to keep these occurrences at bay and, certainly, from destroying your confidence in yourself. Isn't it time you stop allowing so-called well-meaning friends and relatives or acquaintances (and yourself) to make you uncomfortable with another alleged "this-is-the-end" infraction and tie you in knots until you become frustrated, agitated, and embarrassed? Isn't it time you considered saying, "Hogwash"? Try these techniques on for size …

What Can I Do When I Don't I Remember the Word For

So you think because you suddenly can't find a word you wanted to use, you are losing it? Another word won't do? Even grabbing a five- or ten-cent word is not an alternative to salve your momentarily distressed ego? Or that you lost your train of thought ... and it will never return. That you may as well give up because your mental acuity is on a decline from which it will not be able to recover? Well, ask yourself again ...

Here is one way to handle this type of situation:

The Five- and Ten-Cent Theory

A simple word choice is useful in this situation. When you have a problem finding a word, when you are having a conversation and the word just doesn't seem to be there: Choose another—any word, even a simple one will do. I call this the five- and ten-cent theory.

This theory comes out of an incident that changed a concept I had held for many decades. When I was in graduate school, my professor was going over an early paper with me. (I had been away from the academic environment for two decades, and he had put himself in charge of the transition of a group of similar students moving into the rigors of academic life.) I had put my whole self into this enterprise; I don't have to tell you how much succeeding here meant to me. One of my personal ideals was the use of big words—so I often stretched. After a wonderful discussion with this very thoughtful and sensitive professor, who told me it was a fine paper (how kind of him!) and discussed all its strengths, he said, "May I make a suggestion? Sometimes, five- and ten-cent words do just fine—they may, in fact, be the better words." Although I often need to remind myself of that lesson, I have never forgotten it. The strange thing, too, is that I have found over the years that those simple words often are better suited to the context. And although I think my professor would be surprised at my use of his lesson at this phase of my life, I think, upon reflection, he would think it most appropriate. And the best part of using a simpler word in the situations where you suddenly feel stuck and can't find the more complex word—you pause too long, perhaps stutter a bit—is that you can take comfort that there is usually a simpler one within reaching distance. In a pinch, any word that comes into your mind will do. You are not writing a masterpiece or entering a school debate where every word matters. As a matter of fact, you can undoubtedly use any old word, with impunity, once you trust the technique and trust yourself. You really can train yourself to do this—just pull a word out of the air if you have to and see how well it works.

Here is another technique to try that fits this issue:

"I'll Think of It in a Minute"

You can do one of two things when you suddenly are faced with a word you can't remember that you feel you should—and know you had. If you have gotten control of your positive thinking attribute and have some success under your belt, this method can work for you; a number of my friends use it. And no, I didn't suggest it: I observed it being used by a dear friend, ten years my junior, whom I have always admired for her articulateness and manner of expressing herself using flawless phrases. She is also blessed with an amazing knowledge base and rarely misses a beat. One day, I noticed something new had come into her speech pattern. This time, there was a slight pause, only slight, followed quickly by, "Oh, I can't think of it. I'll think of it in a minute"—and she kept on going, with her lovely smile leading the way. In so doing, she had reduced this potential horror to nothing—no importance attached at all. Since she had attached little significance to her momentary departure, so did I! So did all the others in the room.

She had realized something important: A conversation does not usually turn on a word, it is the story you are telling, the point you are making, the thesis you are expounding—not the failure to find (or a momentary loss of) a word—that is important! This bears a moment of thought, does it not? More than a moment, perhaps—because it can make a huge difference to you in how well you handle those momentary lapses of thought or word. And besides, if you never get back to that word, or name, or place that didn't come at that moment, what nice person is going to remind a friend, anyway? If they do— well, you should ask yourself: How nice are they really being? And act accordingly! Practice that technique until you are comfortable with it; it depends on so few words: "I'll think of it in a minute." Again, not difficult, no extra skill required, yet it is extremely helpful in getting past that moment, potentially destructive to the ego. It is worth trying. My friend now leaves out the first part of the response entirely: She finds "I'll think of it in a minute" just as effective or more so—and keeps on going.

Postscript

I once witnessed Winston Churchill's daughter, Sarah, during a televised book review, have one of these moments. Sweetly, with no diminution of her confidence showing, and with a lovely smile, she said to her audience, "I'm having one of those senior moments." Everyone laughed, while she looked off for a few seconds and resumed her talk. Who knows if she had caught the thought or let it go and went on to another? I didn't, and the applauding audience made no noticeable negative sign that they had or that they had even noticed. She had accepted it—a normal physiological change of maturing people—and so, it seemed, had they, partly because she may have had others of her age group in the audience, who recognized the problem; but also, in good part, by her acceptance of the change. One other important aspect of this particular situation: She treated it naturally. Perhaps that is the best lesson of all for those of the Silver Generation.

Here is a third choice:

"I See It, I Know It, I Describe It"

The third way I have found useful in situations where the word or thought gets lost works quite nicely, too. If I can't find the word I want quickly, but I can see an image related to the word in my mind's eye (so frustrating!) and I am getting uncomfortable with the time lapse, I start to describe it. For example, I say, "The tree we saw on our walk to the _____"; or "the movie playing at the cinema in _____"; or "the piece that was on the dresser in ____ house." Born out of desperation, this method is an alternative that works surprisingly well.

A fascinating concomitant result is that, most often, by the time I have finished the description, the "WORD" has magically reappeared in my mind. So I have a double or triple bonus: I don't make a fool of myself (or think I've made a fool of myself) tripping over a word I should have immediately known, and I don't miss a beat. More importantly, perhaps, I continue my train of thought and conversation without the raised eyebrows, without the knowing looks passing between the people I am talking with, and without the interruption to my conversation—the one I wanted to have before the word got in the way. Yes, the potential embarrassment and loss of confidence I might readily feel in such a situation is unpleasant, but I have come to realize the greater loss, really, is to me: not the loss of face, but the loss of thought.

Another unexpected reward for me has been that suddenly I find people interested—maybe more interested—in the description than they might have been in the exact word I thought I needed. A bonus indeed! As to which of these to choose, that will be up to you: The techniques chosen should be based on your level of comfort, your natural way of dealing with situations, and certainly your preference. Experiment with what you feel might work for you—and then try it!

What Can You Do When You Lose a Train of Thought?

Much of the preceding discussion applies to the "train of thought" issue as well; however, there are a few significant factors that need to be discussed separately regarding this issue. Most often, a train of thought is lost when you are interrupted. The easiest way to resolve this issue is not to let it happen, to nip it in the bud. Usually, it occurs when someone interrupts or has a burning question or diversion that he or she feels must be heard at that moment. The key to stopping this behavior is to recognize it and NOT TO LET IT HAPPEN! Offset it! Divert it! Stop it! That is my advice. My son shakes his head when he is about to be interrupted: a positive acknowledgment that the person wants to say something on the subject, while at the same time he puts up his hand in a restraining gesture like a police officer at a crossing. This implies, without words or allowing an interruption, "Yes, I see you agree or have a point to make—but hold it!" If the person interrupts anyway, he says gently—well, maybe not always that gently—but firmly, "Wait! Let me finish!" And he doesn't pause for breath. This usually works. This is the best technique I know. Although my son is not entering that age, this technique is on target, as are many of the ordinary courtesies of communication that used to be taught (if not practiced) more often.

For the ones who try to interrupt by saying, "Can I just ask you a question?" (I love that one!), you must state firmly, "Wait until I am finished, please." Then there are the others with a similar tendency to blurt something out that seems to need immediate addressing. (Think of a three-year-old.) You think you can easily respond and get on with or back to your thought, only to find that you can't get back on track or don't remember where you were. (How many times have you allowed yourself to be fooled by that one?) Maybe you could do this with ease at an earlier stage in your life, or in certain environments and not others, but you will find it more difficult to do at this stage. So again, what else is new? Try to remember, in these situations: People shouldn't interrupt anyway; it is rude. (More will be said on this particular situation in Chapter 13 on Intimidation Management.)

When All Else Fails

What follows are some suggestions for when all else fails. Although they may not get you back on track, they will make you feel better—or, at least, allow you to get out of a situation with your ego intact:

Share the Blame Technique: "What was I saying?" (No response!) "I guess you weren't too interested anyway?" (This last part has the added punch—which you can consider is deserved.) Turn to another subject or another person.

Standard Approach: "I'll think of it in a minute." If you don't, consider going on to something else, or pause and let someone else take over—but don't apologize!

Shift the Attention (sweetly, plus …): "I've lost the thought; well, interruptions tend to do that. Perhaps you'd save your remarks or questions for after I've finished next time?"

The Chastising Approach*:* "I know you are dying to get your thoughts in, but I'm dying to finish my thought first. Okay?" And move quickly on: The problem here may be that by the time you finish chastising the interrupter, you have lost the thought. You can cover this by the following response:

The Annoyed, Exasperated Response: "Never mind. You go right ahead." And give whatever gracious unkind gesture comes to mind—a bow with flourish makes your point quite dramatically, and if this is (or can be) your style, use it by all means.

Postscript

Finally, a note: If you have lost it, you have lost it. Eventually your experience will give you the confidence that the thought will come back. DON'T BEAT UP ON YOURSELF! If, however, the thought suddenly pops into your head when someone else is talking (despite what I have said about interrupting others), don't hesitate to interrupt: You have earned this right—especially if the person speaking is the one who interrupted you in the first place. Egos are fragile things, and self-respect is nothing to be toyed with at any age! If you have lost it because someone interrupted, you can say, "Okay, I've got it and I'm taking the floor now." Can you do it? Sure you can—turnabout is fair play, now, isn't it? Besides, one of the benefits of being of the Silver Generation is you generally won't be stopped if you are firm—age has its advantages. Go with it.

Concluding Remarks:

If you listen, you will hear people of all ages constantly say, "I lost my train of thought" or "I was going to say something—don't remember what at the moment." Or more often now, I hear people say, "What is the word for ...?" If you can get hold of this fact, you will make life much easier for yourself. Don't beat up on yourself; remember: It isn't only those entering that age who find this happening; it happens to people at all ages. Bear that in mind! So, if all else fails, you can simply let it go (probably the hardest, but maybe the easiest under some circumstances).

In summation: Choose the techniques that seem most comfortable to you first, but try some of the others. You may surprise yourself: They may not seem that uncomfortable at all—but rather surprisingly empowering (a concept dealt with more fully in Part II). Knowing what to do and having the tools at hand is quite liberating—but more importantly, it creates the environment you need to fully participate in the life that you want. Remembering that, you will be able to get over any hurdles you might feel exist at this time by using techniques and strategies that accomplish your purpose. Gaining control and taking charge are important at any stage of life. It is very important after you enter that age because at that point, it is a quality-of-life factor: yours!

Chapter 8

PAST PANIC: TAKING CHARGE

Examining Loss and Gaining a Perspective

You have been all too willing to play a game that more and more does not comport with scientific and medical fact. If your goal is to maximize your opportunities in this age of expanding opportunities for full participation in the world you live in—your world—then your inquiry must simply be: "How can I take control of situations that interfere with furthering my own interests and development?" "How can I break away from the fears and panic, push aside the concerns of entering that age by handling them?" Get on with your life—rich in possibilities.

Changing the Pattern in Social Situations

How important is the memory loss we have been discussing in the scheme of things anyhow? What gains are you forfeiting to get a passing grade in this one? What areas of your own dynamic interest and excitement are you repressing ("Oh, who would be interested, anyway?") and failing to share? Yes, there are losses as you enter that age: You see it, you feel it, and you cannot deny it. There is no attempt to do so here: We lose cells as we grow older; in particular, and noticeably, we lose brain cells that relate to memory—mostly short-term memory. But it has been stressed throughout Part I of this book how, with minor adjustments and common sense, you can easily compensate for strange new patterns cropping up. (And of course, you do want to compensate: You can't forget about the pot of water on the stove; you'd rather not spend endless hours looking for something; you'd prefer to remember why you went into a room—more often than not. Of course you would—and can!)

Further, you have also seen that this Silver Generation has enormous allies marching right alongside: Scientific, medical, and technological advances are racing ahead to minimize the effects of short-term memory loss. If you have been putting some of the strategies and techniques suggested in earlier chapters into action, regarding Debunking Myths and Debunking More Myths II, you know that many of these issues are readily addressable: Compensate! Learn the new techniques and strategies! Handle the situations! In other words, deal with these issues!

As long as you can get these bothersome nuisances under control, you may have begun to realize that they are not really that important, at this juncture—not enough to panic! And by now, you should be realizing: You can gain control through compensation and other strategies and techniques! Yes, the changes are part of normal aging that comes with the territory, but which you do not have to allow to become life-altering—at least, they do not have to be. You should understand at this point that dealing with these annoyances is certainly in the realm of probability.

You have been all too willing to play a game that more and more does not comport with scientific and medical fact. If your goal is to maximize your opportunities in this age of expanding and endless opportunities for full participation in the world you live in—your world—then your inquiry should simply be: How can you take control of such social situations and further your own interests and development? Can you better restructure these social situations so that they are more positive experiences for you? Can you understand and accept the difficulties of memory loss (you lose some short-term memory cells, but you can compensate)? Can you understand and accept the difficulties of memory loss as a normal part of the life expectancy? Can you change the situations in which these shortcomings are most evident (where you are apt to suffer loss of esteem, humiliation, and embarrassment) into genuine gain? Can you, in other words, take charge in social situations where you find yourself becoming embarrassed or anxious, or feel you are under attack? I genuinely believe you have the skills, knowledge, and abilities to do so—or that you can readily acquire them.

Why Change the Present Patterns?

Let us spend a few moments, then, getting past the fear and embarrassment, past the unease and intimidation (dealt with more fully in Part II), past both the "It isn't happening" and the "You can do enough about it to mitigate the damage" aspects and focus instead on how you can get through and past these moments that are dragging some of you down so unmercifully (and filling you with unfounded panic!). Let's concentrate instead on why you should bother learning these strategies and techniques: Why you should spend the time, effort, and energy on learning and practicing how to turn these situations around—what exactly are the gains to be made, anyway?

Challenging those terrible social situations and getting on top of them is, of course, a primary goal. Obviously, you do not want to feel that you are losing it as you enter that age. But if you can alter those everyday, important, but fairly mundane tasks with minimal effort and concentrate your energies on more positive things that will not only bring more pleasure and satisfaction, but also put you in better control of your life—the life you want—what joy that would bring! It is time to throw off the unrealistic shackles of those who would tie you to an outmoded past (no longer applicable to this time and place—if it ever was) and take a different approach and gain a new perspective by eliminating the unnecessary time and energy needed to concentrate on the mundane issues discussed in Debunking Myths and Debunking More Myths II, and now here in Debunking More Myths III. Let's look further at what those altered states might allow you after you have entered that stage—by taking a different approach.

Altered States

What Do You Really Want From Social Situations

Wouldn't you rather concentrate on what you thought yesterday than what you ate? Perhaps, like me, you have started to mull over wider and deeper questions and thoughts such as: Is this country, land of the free and home of the brave, in decline? Everywhere we look, something seems to have gone wrong. What is the history of the few great democracies, Greece and Rome, for example? Were their "rises" meteoric and their "declines" swift? Is that where we are, or can we pull it out? Or on another completely different, more personal track, "I look in the mirror and she is there, I comb my hair and she is there—Am I my mother; is she me?"[8] Is that all bad? Will some of me be carried within my granddaughter—is it already?" (Some of you may remember the song from the play *On a Clear Day*, with Barbara Harris, when one of the characters lingers over the prospect: "When I will be born again"— what a grand and poignant moment.) Or a thought grounded more in the present: Was this past election really just about power and gender and race struggles? Is that what it was? Will we ever be truly able to put our biases and smallness aside? Are we all shackled by conditioning,

---

8   From *Fear, Trembling & Renewal: Poems to Age With,* by Norma Roth.

or is it possible that someday reason can prevail? On a totally different vein: "Can I find contentment in the beauty I have surrounded myself with: the mountains, the sea, the green of the landscape, the sunset, and ignore the world? Can one do that? Can I? Should one do that? Should I? Well, maybe only a respite then." Of course, you have your own special thoughts related to your own sphere of interests, your own background, your own life and pursuits, don't you?

What Were Your Thoughts Today?

What were your thoughts today? The ones you squelched; the ones that floated through your mind for an instant—and you let it go? What might you have thought about if you allowed yourself the moment to "drift"? Yes, drift! Absentmindedly perhaps, but oh my, how interesting that might be: Perhaps you will reach into another base of knowledge within that you have not touched upon for years; perhaps a partly memorized poem comes to mind that you can look up later, or a field of study you loved, learned, but have not returned to dwell upon for such a long time … drifting through your mind as you walk along. Or if you took that walk, or carried that book, or looked at an image around you and let your mind take it in and mull over it or even run with it—what might you have thought?

What might you have wanted to share? Did you write something in your journal—and actually read to a friend or relative, or talk about it instead of some topic of no interest or importance to you? Perhaps you allowed yourself, once again, to fall into the pattern of what I call the vagaries of social discourse: "How are you? What's up? What did you eat today? Did you remember to take your pills?" (which kind relatives invariably manage to slip back into the conversation). And your almost catatonic responses: "How is Joyce—what term is she in now? Where are you and John going on vacation? Did you have a good time last year—where were you? I forget." All of which, by the way, may well feed into the self-fulfilling unwanted reports of bits and fragments of your conversations to others that you are so concerned about—and should be: "She can't even remember where we were last year, she asked the same question about Jane, and didn't remember what term her own granddaughter is in"—and the irony is that you already knew most of the answers, didn't you? Aren't you often just making small talk? So the answers: "Great, she's a sophomore, didn't I tell you? John's so busy, you know, still busy. I'm going shopping for a cruise; I don't know what to wear!" And back to you: "How did you spend your day?" (Think of all the interesting conversations you might have exchanged for these communications that pass for conversations!) And do you, like so many of the Silver Generation, respond, when someone asks, "How did you spend your day?" or "What did you do?" with one of the many other vagaries of social discourse? "Oh, nothing special ... just the same routine—you know."

You should no longer be willing to give up potentially interesting conversations. You should no longer be willing to trade the potential of a really interesting conversation for the social niceties and amenities you think are so important—not to mention how they trip you up with their often inane memory quizzes. If you think of it, aren't these fragments of conversation just a bit—maybe a lot—boring and redundant, too?

Make These Moments Work for You; Really Sharing Your Thoughts

Why don't you share those other thoughts? You know; the deeper ones you had while walking or reading or drifting—or even the so-called unfolding events you might have caught on the news if you had the radio or television on, news that perhaps was of interest to you or you wanted to discuss further? Why don't you share those thoughts, ask those questions? There is no better time in your life to establish new lines of communication based on your interests and your thoughts. This is the time for you to build new pathways, to channel conversation and communication more to your liking. You really don't want your life to flit by with trivia (of course, you want news about your grandchildren's and your children's lives ... but how much and when to stop?). And what do you care to remember of these events, anyway? Some things, but not others; maybe not a lot of other conversations, if you were truthful with yourself.

Can't you say, after an interval or when you are asked about your day, "I was thinking about_____ today; what do you think?" Of course you can. Or simply, "Tell me about that book you are reading," perhaps adding that you would like to borrow it, leaving the potential for a further conversation on an interesting subject for you, should you wish to pursue it. That would be a good start to your next encounter: any problem with that?

Taking Charge

Yes—there is a world of ways in which you can carve out a niche for yourself—change, alter, shape patterns more to your own liking and move conversations to your own interests (a double gain: avoid nonsense conversations, the conversation stoppers that put you in a hole—while revitalizing the moment with something good: something you love and want to talk about or do). You can do it! You have the skills, the abilities, the knowledge base, the experience, the wisdom, and the motivation—don't let anyone tell you differently! Put yourself in charge! You stand to gain, not lose, as science continues to open new paths to healing that will embrace both your physical being and mental faculties. The path is before you—if you will only seize it. Be confident of your future: use it! Do the same with music or poetry—or whatever you are interested in. Get used to the phrase, "Let me read you something" or "Let me share a piece of music I've just rediscovered." Or to our computer-literate grandchildren: "I am thinking about this composer or that author, the title of the piece is something like ____; the lines that come to mind are ___. Can you see if you can Google it for me?" (This means to research it on the Internet, like we looked through pages of a book or file cards in libraries for hours on end, but now, it takes them so little time—even seconds sometimes.) You will have a wonderful source for almost instant information and maybe a good conversation as well. I do this with one of my grandchildren now; it works well. And I may even make a breakthrough in the use of the computer—one of these days: find a comfort zone with computer use. I feel it coming—at least at moments, I do. In this proliferation of this extraordinary tool of the twenty-first century, few things if mastered or learned how to navigate better, I suspect, may give those entering that age a greater sense of accomplishment.

Isn't it time you shared your world with friends and family? If your interests are like mine (literature, art, music), don't you think it even more important to share your world with them—especially if it is music and literature, which seem, at the moment, to have been put on a back burner due to the focus on science/biology/medicine/engineering (which I am not at all criticizing, just noting). Shakespeare certainly can still creep into many aspects of life: politics, history, ethics, human relationships, and war: "And gentlemen in England now a-bed/Shall think themselves accurs'd they were not here ... That fought with us upon Saint Crispin's day" (*King Henry V*, the Battle of Agincourt). Does this battle—one of many in the Hundred

Years' War—tell us much of the promises and failures of all wars? Or Shylock's words in *The Merchant of Venice*: "If you prick us, do we not bleed?" (which may say more about the absurdities of prejudice than many written treatises). Or Hemingway's use of John Donne's "Do not ask for whom the bell tolls." Learn to pull out those notebooks or that one-volume Shakespeare. Or pull from the shelf those leather-bound books of poetry you loved, which you meant to read, and read; don't allow those beloved books to continue languishing on those shelves. Start today—see how many poems and lines of poetry you remember: stored away in your memory (bring them into focus—yours). Or when a line of poetry comes your way, learn to Google that poem. Nothing gives greater instantaneous pleasure than to have unfolded before you the full lines and stanzas of a poem you dearly love—and only remember a few lines. (What a magnificent use of the computer!)

Recently, I sent a book of poetry to a young friend; she sent me back a note on the Dylan Thomas lines I had used at the beginning of a poetry book: "Do not go gentle into that good night/Old age should burn and rave at close of day/Rage, rage against the dying of the light." She sent me back a quote on age and dying; I did not know it. I put the line into Google and in moments, the entire poem it came from appeared, in large print too. I printed it and will bring it to lunch—which we mean to do soon, my young, wise friend of forty-five, and we will talk some more. I am looking forward to it.

Over the summer, I had the opportunity to share an aspect of my world with my grandson. He had brought his iPod and played it through my Bose. I was amazed, it was magic to hear the quality of that radio playing from his small, new, magical gadget, and lest you think there could not be a mutual exchange—how, after all, can I keep up with all the technological changes—there was. I had just rediscovered a whole host of 33½ RPM recordings (remember those?). And I just happened to have an old record player (which we called a "Victrola," as some of you may admit remembering, too). My grandson pulled out one of my long-playing records he apparently knew, and when I told him he could put it on, he said, "Wow, now I can learn how this works?" meaning the old reliable phonograph with a diamond needle that still did its superb job—or almost. Of course that has its moment of truth, but it also has an endearing interaction. Will wonders never cease? Well, we won't know if we allow ourselves to be dropped out of the world or do it to ourselves, now, will we?

Ask yourself as you travel on the journey throughout this book: How important is it to you how many times you walk into a room—if you can take your thoughts with you or perhaps work through more meaningful conversations you might like to have—if you can compensate for lack of concentration on the task at hand? How important if your thoughts—the ones that, at times, make you seem absentminded—stay with you no matter what room you are in, if they take you back to moments of professional pride and past accomplishment, if you can routinize your tasks sufficiently so you don't encounter a serious problem with the task at hand? Or how important when suddenly you can continue working your mind around an aspect of your private world that you loved and hadn't thought much about as you lived through life, but now can reflect upon—if you can stay in the kitchen while you are boiling water for pasta? Which is more important to you? To think about what you had for breakfast because so-and-so is coming or calling, or to continue these weightier and more personally worthwhile thoughts—ESPECIALLY IF YOU CAN COMPENSATE for those short-term memory losses! Only you can decide.

Concluding Remarks

Have I made my point? Yes, you have issues to deal with as a result of your entering that age: It comes with the territory. When you take into account the multitude of better conversations, more meaningful exchanges, expansion of interests and ideas that can come out of the thinking pattern described above, you might begin to suspect that things are not what they seem: You stand to gain a great deal with the help of science speeding along in its research studies of the brain, how it functions, how it repairs, how it remains clear, and how you can better ensure that all pathways are fully functional.

When you consider the potential from taking charge, being in control of the direction of conversations, filling the social environment with the sounds of you, perhaps it will not be all that difficult to accept the difficulties of some memory loss as a normal part of the aging process and let the scourge of that short-term memory loss go: Let it go as the wisps of clouds disappear on the horizon—let it go and live your own life to the fullest that life can possibly be lived and suffer no fools lightly.

Do I make my point? Once you become aware of the hogwash of so-called telltale signs of losing it, once you have put into practice the simple methods to offset the natural losses that take place (but are not life-altering), once you put behind you (the quicker, the better!) those exaggerated concerns triggered by outmoded social mores, perhaps into the nearest garbage disposal, you will free yourself to go along a different and far better path: one that includes the dazzling light of scientific and medical discoveries that offer enormous benefits for the Silver Generation.

Once you get these concerns behind you, you will be ready to move on to a far more exciting, expansive, and exhilarating part of the potential ability of your brain's long-term memory and other banks, pathways to which are unfolding in great ways every day and every way. Worth the effort? You decide. As you go through your day, you control your world and your time. Wherever you are; whatever room in the house; whatever place outside—you decide whether to go or not, whether to stop or stay, whether to look out one window or another, whether, as Plato urges, you "come … into the light." You are the center of your universe. Which window will you choose to look out on the world, your world? You decide. Take control!

Remember: This is your life; use it—and don't let anyone take it from you prematurely! Make your world—your life—what you want it to be, or at least try.

I end this chapter by sharing a journey with you:

"Letting Go"

I am tired of raised eyebrows:
They do not ask me what my thoughts are
they do not ask me how I see life today
they do not ask me what I would like to do
where I would like to go, what goals I have

"Past Panic"

I still have hopes
I still have dreams
and I am wise
My goals are many

My dreams are infinite
My intention is to live fully!

(from *Fear, Trembling & Renewal: Poems to Age With*, © 2009 Norma Roth)

PART II

THE AGE OF THE SILVER GENERATION BEGINS

- Treasures

- Your Personal Retrieval System (PRS)

- Empowerment

Introduction

THE AGE OF THE SILVER GENERATION BEGINS

The Great Gifts to the Silver Generation

The twenty-first century may be the Age of the Silver Generation, the age where how far you go may only be limited by your imagination, creativeness, and innovation. The magic of the century is the limitless possibilities being handed to this dynamic generation on a "silver" platter. All that is needed is the confidence, the spunk, and the individuality—and sometimes the defiance to walk along those new pathways opening and to blaze the trails awaiting. This generation has a rendezvous with destiny as no other ... you will need to understand the art of empowerment. Part II of this book, dear reader, is for you ...

While Part I of this book was based on the question of recognizing, preventing, and compensating for changes that normally take place as one enters that age, and the societal factors that make that entrance and the pursuit of a fuller life more burdensome, Part II changes the terrain. This part is devoted to what you can do to enhance your existing strengths, develop your hidden treasures, and build upon resources within to utilize skills and a knowledge base within the self, of which you will become more fully aware. The next few chapters, drawing upon a new paradigm based on the educational model, will introduce you to treasures you have just below the surface and to the rich potential within yourself that I call a Personal Retrieval System (PRS). Based on what you have retained and what science is unraveling about long-term memory, I present my thoughts on the enormous potential that lies in wait for you. Further, I take you on an exciting journey within the self.

As Part I of this book passed from exposing the socialization factors that are fast becoming obsolete, past hurdles faced by previous generations entering that age, your outlook was being greatly broadened. You will be able to focus more completely on the positive steps to capitalize on your strengths, move on to treasure hunts for known and partially developed areas of interests, and re-explore and build on an already existing universe of yourself.

In Chapter 10, Treasure Hunts, I entice you to re-enter your world of former loves: interests and pursuits attempted, but dropped somewhere along the way. I suggest that by picking up on interests you long ago intended to pursue, but didn't, or started and stopped, you will not only extend your resources, but also, by drawing and building on them, quickly feel smarter. In Chapter 11, Personal Retrieval Systems, a new treasure is unfurled, perhaps a more difficult resource to access, but as you will quickly understand, it is a major retrieval system within the self. Hence, it cannot help but be a richly rewarding discovery. (I suspect many of you already access your PRS, to some extent, knowingly or not. However, I believe the accessibility and the wide application of this system, particularly to those entering that age, have not been fully explored.) Consider this a treasure hunt of a deeper nature, one that can lead you to a vast (albeit previously misunderstood, but fully developed) body of knowledge. Your Personal Retrieval System has the potential of unleashing a magnificent system: The sum total of your life experiences and knowledge base, a system that includes much of what you learned throughout your life and much of what you have become (your experience)—and which is both accessible and, in large part, retrievable; while treasure hunts take you down paths known before but, perhaps, never fulfilled to the extent you might have wished.

If you still have doubts about the importance, in the scheme of things, of the issues discussed in Debunking Myths in Part I, most of which involve short-term memory loss, it will become even more abundantly clear in the next few chapters that if you take steps to compensate for the effects of any short-term memory loss, in the long run, the losses you may fear count for very little when there are such bountiful mental treasures awaiting you in that other part of your brain, long-term memory banks, where you have stored knowledge, experience, and more over a lifetime.

While short-term memory has only limited capacity and brief duration (which means that information is available for a certain period of time and is not retained indefinitely), long-term memory, in contrast—which was briefly discussed in the previous chapters on the educational process—can store much larger quantities of information for potentially unlimited duration, maybe a whole life span. Part II explores a new paradigm: As science and medicine find ways to ensure that the pathways to those long-term memory banks are made available to those entering that age, you may well be able to draw upon all that knowledge previously learned. It becomes the educational model that will come into prominence in this century. It is time for a new paradigm that suits the new developments. Part II explores an educational paradigm that comports with the findings of science and advancements in medicine anticipated in this century—and already occurring. How exciting a development for members of this generation to consider that the whole panoply of data acquired over a lifetime may well be accessible. Under the right conditions, members of the Silver Generation, you may well be able to access and retrieve information for almost your entire life span. Hence, Part II introduces the educational paradigm.

Empowerment, too, is an essential aspect of Part II of this book; empowerment is another way of taking charge of the situations that face those entering that age. It is the awareness that rights that you have (or should have) are being impeded or trampled upon; it is the recognition that you empower yourself when you say, "I will not allow it, and I will do what I must to ensure that I am treated with respect." After all, it is your world, too, and you do not intend to allow false hurdles and obstacles to be thrown your way. It is that confidence with which you empower yourself, and that willingness of aging defiantly, that gives you the powerful tools for charting your own course. It is the empowerment that can be used to manage such inappropriate social behaviors as intimidation, a social behavior that can inhibit the full participation of those entering that age. A little more tricky to handle, perhaps—but once understood, it can be handled. As in many things, it is the recognition, the understanding, and the will that will enable you to manage the issues that those entering that age encounter. In Part II, you will be assisted by old friends Marty (from the delightful movie with Ernest Borgnine) and Cyrano from the play many of you are familiar with, *Cyrano de Bergerac* (who fortunately gives us twenty ways to ward off those who would dare to intimidate), and, yes, even some older friends: the Girl Scouts or Boy Scouts, whose motto, you may recall, is "Be Prepared."

The best thing about these chapters is that they deal with growth— your growth and the rich potential that lies within this already amazing generation. Empowerment, you will come to understand, will enable you to more fully participate in a world more of your making, more of your design, and more comfortable and satisfying to you as you chart your own course, as you begin to move down the path of new treasure hunts and concentrate on your own personal base of knowledge within your Personal Retrieval System.

As you renew your acquaintance with the wonderful resources available to you within yourself, much of it from data stored in your long-term memory system, the amazing potential for continued and active intellectual involvement will be immediately apparent. Part II, dear readers, is for you. All that is needed is the confidence, the spunk, and the individuality—and sometimes the defiance—in order to walk along those new pathways opening up and to blaze the trail that is waiting for this Silver Generation.

Chapter 9

INTRODUCING A NEW PARADIGM

Unfolding the Renaissance Person of the Twenty-First Century

Science, Medicine, Education, and the Computer Age Come to the Aid of the Silver Generation

> The Renaissance Woman has been my goal, NOT a feeble person losing her mind. I wondered why and whether the pedagogy of yesteryear might not be more applicable to the present ... especially in view of the remarkable advancements of science, medicine, and technology opening limitless possibilities to the Silver Generation—for both body and mind. I decided to put present societal concepts as an influence to rest and embrace a different model that has served me well all my life.

Educational Process Redux; Social Attitudes Discarded!

In the Preface, I voiced the absurdity of all absurdities to me that at the very moment when I seemed ready to bring all my thoughts, ideas, and philosophic probing together, to think seriously about all the bits and pieces that have been working their way through my mind all these years on myriad subjects, I found myself facing a crisis: Societal attitudes and behaviors were not with me. The accepted patterns of aging to which I was expected to conform stood in stark contradiction with these long-sought-after and looked-forward-to goals. In fact, I found it more and more unsettling as I came face to face with what appeared on the horizon as an absolute: the prospect of the aging process as an inevitable loss of cells, and consequently inevitable and irretrievable memory loss, or so I was told. In short, what this meant, of course, was that the stimulating mental, intellectual life I had envisioned for myself was over—forget it. The prevailing concept permeating the air was, if you can get through a day without burning the house down, consider it a miracle. I have come a long way in my thinking since then to begin to get a better perspective on the aging process, and the ability to compensate for many of the so-called signs of losing it, which I shared with you in Part I of this book.

Before I continue with Part II where the focus shifts to your strengths, your possibilities, and the vast horizons that lie waiting, many of which may well be yours for the taking, I want, for a moment, to return to my thoughts on the pedagogical theories that I suggested earlier: the educational process through which you learned—and are learning still—as a better model for those entering this Age of the Silver Generation. I want to present more fully a positive and exciting paradigm for the Silver Generation that makes more sense in light of present confluence of science and medicine, the dynamism and life expectancy of those entering that age, and the methodology of learning that so many of us have been exposed to over a lifetime. After all, this new century promises no less than limitless fulfillment of anticipated goals and dreams well into a life expectancy now rising into the eighties and nineties.

As I started out by saying in the beginning of this journey, the irony of a concept of losing it at the very moment of greatest maturity did not escape me. I spoke earlier of the senselessness, absurdity, and irony of being targeted to spend potentially the richest of my years out to pasture, where I definitely foresaw little or no chance for fulfillment of my goals and dreams. Simultaneously, in view of continued advances in life expectancy, on an almost day-by-day basis, the truthfulness of these societal attitudes and behavioral mannerisms being pushed at me took on a sense of ludicrousness. I understand quite clearly that like myself this dynamic, new generation of this twenty-first century wanted more, expected more, and would have more! More and more, I was thinking that what was being postulated by societal norms for those entering that age at this time, at this place, at this juncture, were boggling to the mind. In fact, the attitudes and behavior patterns, with the crystal-clear inference that irretrievable loss of mental faculties facing those entering that age, and hence the rocking chair/out-to-pasture syndrome made less and less sense every single day.

What exactly would I be losing? What exactly would this Silver Generation be losing? With all the marvels of science, medicine, and technology surrounding and tantalizing those entering that age, the expectations were high—very high. Loss of cells? Neuroscience was telling us that changes in aging do not include widespread neuron loss. Nor is intelligence relying on learned or stored information suffering a significant decline. Further, neuroscience[9] is now telling us the brain can remain relatively healthy and fully functioning as it ages. So why should the expectations of the Silver Generation not be high? Of course

---

9   I have used a variety of sources for information in this book regarding scientific and medical research studies. The material in this section has been based primarily on data gathered by the Society for Neuroscience ("Brain Facts") and recent articles from Harvard University, Cornell University, Brown University, University of Pennsylvania, and MIT, all of which are engaged in fascinating research and developments in this area, as well as scientific journals. I reiterate that my book is not a scholarly journal, but rather one of an educated person, lawyer, and educator entering that age. I have listed a short bibliography at the conclusion of this book.

they should. When research is indicating that other causes like diseases, stress, nutrition, and lack of exercise come into play regarding loss of mental acuity—and this is not an irretrievable loss—why should those entering that age not have high expectations? Of course they should! Increasingly, but persistently, annoyance, irritation, and anger were overcoming and replacing fear, panic, and excessive concern.

Again, thinking about all I already had learned, the time I spent learning and relearning—highlighting the purpose of that methodology of teaching: to put the information learned (data) into our minds (store data) for continued usage (access) throughout most of our lifetime as needed (retrieval)—a neon sign appeared in my mind. I felt a Broadway moment had arrived—the Broadway of the time when Rogers and Hammerstein were key and the grand musicals lit up my life! Juxtaposing the remarkable, unheralded, and rapid advancement of science, medicine, and technology in the field of aging, the societal attitudinal influence fell by the wayside: It was a hoax. One would have to be slightly off balance not to see these advancements as an enormous gain. Such a negative view of limited potential as one ages was finally totally unacceptable when compared to the realization that a lifetime of learning and expectations, a lifetime of overachieving, of overdoing, and of acquiring so much knowledge in all different areas that had been the driving force in my life need not be wasted.

I really needed little more convincing, at this point, that the "this-is-the-way-it-is, accept it" attitude of losing it permeating the societal milieu toward those entering that age was wrong! Big time! And that the educational process through which we learned—and are learning still—is a better model for those entering this Age of the Silver Generation. Given the gifts that lay before us, overwhelmingly rich with possibilities not even clearly understood in terms of the far-reaching potential of those entering that age, the Silver Generation stood rather on the threshold of a very bright new day indeed.

Clearly, such a bright new world called for an equally bright new model, emitting and reflecting the silver glitter of the new generation. The Renaissance Woman, the Renaissance Man—NOT a feeble person losing her or his mind—would be my model yet! I considered that the pedagogy of yesteryear was a far more suitable underpinning for this Silver Generation. Further, it would be a far more applicable model, given all these remarkable changes and possibilities on the horizon for those entering that age. I almost needed no more convincing, at this point, that the social influences were obsolete.

There were other theories being advanced also: one being discussed in the halls of medical offices and between researchers and neuroscientists as well: the "Use It or Lose It" possibility of brain function, and another theory advanced in the eighties and nineties that came to my attention. It was so bold, so ahead of its time in looking directly at the question of involvement in old age, I felt both supported in challenging a conflicting world that was facing me and greatly encouraged with the exploration I had made and the road I was traveling.

Another Voice Heard From: *The Life Cycle Completed*

In their two books on aging, *Vital Involvement in Old Age* and *The Life Cycle Completed,* noted psychoanalyst Erik H. Erikson and his wife Joan M. Erikson, along with Helen Q. Kivnick, began to see the older years as simply another stage, the next phase of carving out a life: new goals, new plans, new ambitions ... but, nonetheless, mostly a full life! I loved the thought: I strongly suspected it was their own life lived into the nineties that gave the Eriksons such passion and insight.

I felt their support reaching out to me as they assert a necessity for a "radical change in our concept of the human life cycle," specifying qualities of experience, wisdom, and integrity endemic to the later stages. Calling the aging population "collectors of time and preservers of memory," asserting the "need to open up our minds to new strategies," and stating "the ultimate capacities of the aging person are not yet determined," what more did I need to discard the outmoded social theories on aging? They did not postulate that people lost it as they aged, not those with healthy bodies and minds, which this generation has in sight; they merely went on into the next cycle of life, where the Eriksons saw wisdom and integrity were lifelong developing processes—Yes!—and forecast contributions that might come as a surprise from this newly emerging group. They also gave short shrift to the inability to learn, another losing process, stating, "There is a rumor abroad that in old age one can no longer learn new skills, new approaches to problems, although this has been disproven repeatedly." (This was from a study done in 1978.)

Would anyone care to comment why it is still so surprising a revelation? Or question why these earlier statements have been so well hidden from us? Neuroscience is just discovering that there may be new cells in the brain available for new learning. A scientific journal (*Scientific American*) recently had an article on this. Doesn't it seem that our society has been greatly remiss in choosing to overlook this valuable resource? (After all, Erik Erikson was only a well-known psychoanalyst and leader in human development—try Pulitzer Prize winner!) Particularly in terms of the attitudes and behavioral mannerisms exhibited in the twenty-first century toward those entering that age, society should be ashamed for holding back and perpetrating these limiting influences. If the Eriksons could see the possibilities "in the not-too-distant future ... healthy, vital old people [would] look forward with anticipation and pleasure to a long life … purposeful involvement as a matter of course," where does that put the social attitudes and the behavior that follow? I leave you to decide. I would say they are a hoax and, definitely, hogwash. The ideas of the Eriksons seem to be leading to the new paradigm as well. When they spoke of the elderly losing some things, but having more wisdom and memory, they corroborated the new paradigm and a knowledge base stored for a lifetime for me.

Why not, indeed, the education model! So much better suited to the times and the lifestyle of this dynamic new group; so much more in sync with the accelerated pace of science and medicine (granting such longevity and health); and so much more suited as well to the theories of these two eminent people, who foresaw this new generation as part of the continuum and developing lifelong process, which might well lead to unknown contributions. My mind became fixed upon the thought. I now saw the "you-are-done-with-this-life" attitude as another hoax—a big one—similar, perhaps, to the one we had passed through about gender limitations: "Biology is destiny," remember that one? Or that other image about men more than seventy being done with an active life! Couldn't be president? Yet, a man more than seventy ran for that high office! A woman at that age can also be expected to run for office sometime in the very near future too. But there was more corroboration for the educational model as a better paradigm.

Another Voice: "Use It or Lose It" Theory

There was another remarkable new theory permeating the environment that was also leading toward this new paradigm: Commonly referred to as the "Use It or Lose It" theory, it has far-reaching and major possibilities for so many of the areas coalescing within science, medicine, education, and psychology.

Recently, I became intrigued, too, by the potential of the "Use It or Lose It" theory. This surfacing theory has great importance for those of the Silver Generation. It advocates the use of your brain, big time. It bears repeating the simple thesis: Use of the brain retains its function; disuse results in loss of its function. The major thrust of this theory cannot be more timely for this dynamic generation in so many different ways related to the forthcoming chapters of this book. The foundations of availability of personal knowledge, skills, and interests you have gained throughout your life—as well as new interests and knowledge that you decide to tackle (yes, you can learn new things)—may well be at your disposal throughout your lifetime.

The major thrust here has been to look back to the foundations of personal knowledge, skills, and interests you have gained throughout your life and to build on them. In this way, not only will you be utilizing your brainpower—the knowledge base you already have—but you will have the opportunity to expand and extend that base wherever you choose to take it, spurred on by both the ongoing findings and further research that is bound to become available on the "Use It or Lose It" hypothesis. Many of the Silver Generation are already embracing it: There is only gain to be had here.

Regardless of what you do with it, there is no doubt you will be using your brain in all of its infinite capabilities—some of which, I am sure, neither you nor science is as yet aware of; all the magnificent possibilities. But by this time, you already have begun to realize, if you had not before, that your generation will be pathfinders and trailblazers. With the addition of this newest gift as well, those entering that age may well reap limitless rewards. A new paradigm is called for.

A New Paradigm

Immensely fortified by the many advances in scientific research regarding the aging brain and those daring to forecast the continuity of the brain functioning as well as highlighting the ability to access long-term memory (the full spectrum of personal knowledge base and experience and more) throughout almost the full life span—and, of course, the developing theory advocating the continued and significant use of the brain throughout your lifetime—it was not difficult to conclude a new paradigm was in order.

The latest theories served as corroboration and impetus to adopt a new paradigm based on an educational model that input knowledge into our long-term memory throughout our lives. Research shows that long-term memory can store large quantities of information for potentially unlimited duration (and the limits of its capacity are not yet known). Others theorize that factual information accumulated over the years remains largely intact, so if it takes a little longer to retrieve, what is the relevance when everything we know about the world may remain within? What a fantastic coalescence of educational pedagogy with scientific, medical, and technological advances that see longevity and health as absolutes for future generations.

What a corroboration of and impetus to all that the Silver Generation desires: to continue living and breathing and thinking; to have brainpower that they will be able to continue to use throughout their lifetime; to know, too, that lifelong learning may well be available to them, and to continue to expand their knowledge base and continue to learn throughout their lives. What more is needed? What a wonderful and potentially rewarding gift: It is not an injection that will be given to you; rather, it is that you will brave the world with the confidence that comes from knowing you have a hidden wealth of brainpower, and that you enhance your own power of the mind by simply using it: no limits, no restrictions, just a universe to explore within and without. So goodbye to all that *nonsense and hogwash discussed in previous chapters.*

No longer need you allow anyone to tell you your mind is ceasing to function, you are losing it, you can no longer learn new facts or at least commit them to memory: You can no longer think! You no longer need to allow others to mislead you with outmoded and fallacious words! Or embarrass you! Or humiliate you! Or make you feel less than you know you are or can be! Or scare you! Or panic you! You become the master of your own fate! Perhaps you would agree with Emerson here when he said, "The only person you are destined to become is the person you decide to be." So my advice is strongly this: ignore those who would put you on a false path. They are wrong—and will lead you on a path you need not take. Modern research is the bearer of better gifts. Sometimes, ideas are the gifts to the world; not gold, not diamonds (but maybe silver!) but ideas. This is one of those true miracle gifts from science and medicine, your stronger allies.

There is the opportunity NOW, in the present, for this dynamic Silver Generation to be in the forefront of revolutionary, exciting areas of mental development of limitless potential. So the theory of retention of learning, storage of learning, retrieval of learning materialized in my mind—not too much of a leap, if you think about it; rather a logical outcome of the remarkable advances of this century. The new paradigm seems eminently more suitable. The fears and concerns about learning or remembering substantive areas, the uncertainty of intelligently discussing or writing about academic areas of the past disappeared: wrong concepts for this age! Wrong conclusions! The new paradigm will serve this Silver Generation far better.

I think about our early educators: Perhaps, they may not have been able to foresee their gifts to this generation, but I think, upon retrospect, as my esteemed English professor from old wrote in his recommendation for me to law school, "that seems like a natural progression." I somehow think these educational theorists would have said the same; after all, certainly they did not go through all those layers of teaching not to anticipate the retention and usefulness of that wide body of knowledge they instilled in each and every one of us for it to disappear like wisps of clouds. They expected it would last forever—and hoped we would use it over an entire lifetime.

The learning methods so long practiced and so dutifully and diligently drilled into our memory banks would and could, indeed, hold us in good stead for the rest of our lives. The educators of the fifties on, like the Eriksons toward the end of the last century, did not fully know where this new age would go, but they certainly knew the possibilities were here and should not be ignored. They also had the vision to see the potential "to seek a new life and role—a new self." And so, this well-equipped Silver Generation shall!

Thenceforth, I would determine my own path—charge ahead regardless of the outcome! It was worth any risk. At this point, I begin to think the risk seems minimal; it is, simply, to move forward in the directions you already know you want to go. Adopting a new paradigm, I believe, so much more suited to the enlarged perspective of each of you, and of the world that is being shaped, will allow you to move more quickly and with more confidence into a bright new future that awaits you...

> *Come, my friends. Tis not too late to seek a newer world*
> *For my purpose holds/To sail beyond the sunset.*
>
> —"Ulysses," Alfred Tennyson

The Educational Paradigm Comes of Age with Assists from Science and Medicine and Psychology

Abandoning the societal aging, "rocking chair," results-oriented model, I turned toward a more positive standard-bearer upon which to model the rest of my life—the educational paradigm—that which I always had, that which I had never left, that which I intended to continue to follow throughout my life. If I were to follow any paradigm, it would be based on the pedagogy I had used for a lifetime, one that allowed those of my generation, who have actually looked forward to entering that age, to move toward the pursuit of personal goals, the fulfillment of dreams, and whatever other wonderful gifts we might find along the way.

How exciting it suddenly feels: all those multiple levels of learning and the probability of a stored knowledge base of great magnitude available, a continuum building upon your knowledge base of all your life. Aren't you glad you studied hard, and thought and spoke or wrote about the things you loved? Learning, forgetting, remembering some, relearning, remembering, forgetting maybe less: an interesting pattern re-emerged in a new light. The possibility that so much of that knowledge might still be present somewhere in the brain cells is exhilarating. Imagine those data bases that may lay dormant waiting for you to use. Just consider for a moment, those weighty substantive areas you learned and memorized and regurgitated and continued going back to on your own as you made your way through life! Waiting, just possibly waiting. Yes, and still waiting! What joy to contemplate! Why not? Waiting: available, retrievable, and usable. Every day, science comes up with brilliant new pathways to those long-term memory resources. Every day, I am more and more convinced that the data base is still available. Life, after all, is a continuum. Especially if, as you went along, some of your memory banks retained more, stored it for you, and made it available to you at other times in your life.

Concluding Remarks

The advances in science and technology that are fast coming into public view do not conflict with, but rather supplement, the theories of education that so many of you have used and continue to use throughout your lives. In fact, science fits into this pedagogical model of learning as smoothly as a silk glove. Numerous neurological studies of the brain indicate that long-term memory is a vast arsenal of stored and retrievable data. The potential seems unlimited as it contains the sum total of your life: both your knowledge base, your experience, and much that may be available that is not yet known. Not to mention the other theory gaining scientific prominence, strongly suggesting those at or entering that age should indeed "use it" (your brain) or "lose it." (Another gift from the gods may be the newest theory coming out of the medical/scientific community regarding another remarkable aspect of the brain (including the aging brain) that postulates that new brain cells might just be available for new learning too.) So much positive scientific and medical underpinnings arriving on the scene enable and empower this brand-new dynamic generation to continue productive lives full of rich potential: certainly a marriage made in heaven.

The Silver Generation Enters a New Renaissance Stage

So I have embraced a different paradigm: Based on a tried-and-tested educational paradigm coupled with rapid advancements in science and medicine—the fulfillment of dreams—it is one that makes eminent sense to me personally, and further, one that offers a paradigm for growth: forever curious, forever seeking, forever learning, forever.

Let us be thankful for gifts. We are thankful for small gifts and large: This seems to be one of those ideas whose time has come; the joining of an idea to a group, a dynamic generation, whose accomplishments are yet unknown. You will be charting your own course—with confidence; you will be taking charge with spunk; and you will be dynamic people at the forefront of dynamic advances of the twenty-first century. Members of the Silver Generation, all you need to do is continue to use your mind, keep on using your mind, never stop using your mind, and you stand to retain its power throughout your lifetime.

Chapter 10

TREASURE HUNTS: EXPLORING OLD AND NEW PATHWAYS

Feeling Smart

Find the treasure within the self; explore old pathways: things you loved and discarded along the way, things you learned but thought you had forgotten, things you stored for another day: there is a treasure awaiting you, and it is there for the taking ... even for the renewing ... even for the adding of new knowledge. To renew and build on an already existing universe within you that is surely a treasure worth seeing ... a self worth becoming reacquainted with.

You Are Smarter Than You Think

This chapter should convince you that you have so much more to give, both to yourself and to others, that with a little effort, you can help yourself to feel and be smarter than social attitudes and behavior patterns may have let you believe. Once you make your way through these treasure hunts and discover, as you are about to, that you may well be the proud possessor of bases of skills, abilities, and knowledge, within the self—you will be motivated. You may come to look at things half learned, some simply put away for another day, some in which you had attained a degree of proficiency, but life got in the way, with new possibilities. Once you find you can access that base, pick up on things you have long loved and lingered over, and continue on, you will feel good. With little notice of the passage of time, you will pick up some of these old areas of interest and begin moving into the stage of feeling smart. So if you are smart—only a small pun intended—you will move quickly in and through the discovery of the self, the discovery of the treasures within the self. You may well emerge with a sense of who you really are and all you really have to give in this dynamic twenty-first century that you may well dominate.

Treasure Hunts: Exploring Old Pathways

In this chapter, hunting for hidden or lost treasures, I want to focus on a process to identify and discover what areas of old and new interests you may want to reexamine, explore, and enjoy. That exploration will take you further down the path filled with the richness of you—a voyage made easier because you have the old foundation upon which to draw (things you had started to explore, skills you had previously developed to a point), and new because you will be building on former interests with the potential for much satisfaction. A wonderful concomitant result of your adventure will be that you will start doing things that make you feel smart, feel satisfied, and feel excited with the potential of life—your life. Additionally, the residual result of reaching into that old storehouse is the way you feel about yourself, the interest you start to take in areas not fully developed before, and the confidence you will feel as a result of "doing your own thing." Can there be a greater feeling?

There are different pathways to learning that you may not yet have fully used, waiting for you to discover them—or rediscover them. I believe that science is slowly moving in the direction of studying many aspects of the brain that until now have been little known or fully understood. Recently, a doctor friend sent me an article that suggests that new brain cells become available to you, even as you age, and are available for new learning. Think of the endless possibilities.

Seeking Buried Treasures Within the Self

It is time to give some thought to those buried treasures: skills, abilities, knowledge bases that have been lying within you, waiting for your commands—the possibilities are endless. Perhaps there was a time you wanted to delve more fully into an aspect of music—perhaps just listening to or, like me, playing pieces of music you love, but didn't get around to—something else always seemed to get in the way. Or you wanted to delve further into the beautiful art that had captured your heart, and didn't (or maybe started but stopped)? Or like me, you let go of that instrument you played and intended to get back to it, but didn't, not even for your own pleasure? Why not pick up and play a piece once in a while on whatever instrument you happened to play: the clarinet, the saxophone, the cello, the violin, the horn? Or pull out those art books or that unused easel still waiting, or go to a museum, or pick up some sketching material? Weren't there lines from great poets that you wanted to remember: Shakespeare, Byron, Shelly, Keats, or a favorite of mine, Elizabeth Barrett Browning? (I recently caught a dramatic reading of her wonderful sonnet "How Do I Love Thee," read by John Lithgow who was being interviewed on WGBH by a person best known for his political commentary. (Yes, even political commentators have other interests!)

Perhaps you wanted to learn favorite lines of bards exciting to you, but haven't quite mastered them yet, or didn't have occasion or confidence to use them—but now you might? What about the great authors you wanted to read or those you did read and marked out passages to reread—when you had the time? I bet some of you still have the books, even tattered copies. This may be a world you have all but forgotten, but once you start to explore, to read or reread those passages or works you loved, you will feel both smarter and, hopefully, motivated to do more. You might even introduce some of your favorites into conversations and dialogues. They will surely add to your interest and excitement about the world around you. You may recall, in Part I, I talked about controlling conversations both to make them more interesting to you and to avoid the traps of senility testing so visible in our society. This might be a great time to do just that. Becoming the change agent for social conversations can add some interest and excitement for you. You will undoubtedly feel better about your contributions, maybe even smarter. How about giving those who would set senility testing traps discussed in Part I of this book something more interesting to think about?

Or how about sports: Didn't you mean to go back and ride that bike of yours or get a newer, easier-to-ride, multi-gearshift model that practically takes off on its own (but gives you enough of a thrill to enjoy the effort until your muscle memory takes over)? Or sailing or tennis (ever hear of brush-up courses: you don't lose the skills)? Two friends of mine, after a hiatus of several years, whipped themselves back into an amazing shape, speed, and dexterity in their tennis skills. (Well, they both were on school teams and ten years younger than me.) Although older and more cautious, I can still say with pride that I am at the best game I have ever been, building slowly but convincingly those skills I labored so hard to learn long ago, but didn't quite get there—until now. No, I don't play as long or run as hard, but I am certainly playing that net well and using my reach, and fortunately for me, my partner is at the same level of physical stamina as I am. So, of course, we have a great game. Finding the right partner for sports is half the battle—but look around: There may be an overabundance of those entering that age just dying to be asked.

With a little encouragement, you might just pick up a good partner, too. Remember, the joy's the thing—and the exercise.

If you do crave intellectual challenge—and how surprisingly often that is—look around. If you are in or near a city or small town, there is a lot going on, especially on new subjects, but they can be enormously interesting. This is the year for Lincoln and Darwin, biological and cell restoration, cartilage regeneration, biomedical engineering, and so much more taking place. You can understand these developments if you put your mind to it, and you can learn from them as well. Think of the interesting discussions that you can have. The possibilities are endless—"as endless as the sea," as the lyrics from an old favorite song remind me. I used to recite a little ditty—long, long ago—to my oldest granddaughter, now in college. I think maybe I was reciting it for myself as well—I find it has applicability for me as I enter that age, too: "For all of my life, I shall always be, myself and no other: Just me."

Expanding Old Pathways; Finding New Treasures: A Personal Experience

I am of the belief that personal experiences often enable others to understand more clearly a concept, so I want to share some experiences of discoveries I have made on some treasure hunts within myself: Not that long ago, I made a trip to Europe to the land of my parents' birth. My parents, immigrants to this country, spoke two languages all of their lives (my mother actually spoke three). To my sister and me, they spoke only English; to each other, they spoke Hungarian. I never learned that language. Not surprisingly, like a lot of other immigrant families coming into the country at that time (in the late 1920s, early 1930s), my parents were running from war, oppression, and poverty. While they retained the language between themselves (because it was easier and more expressive for them; they had enough to adjust to in a new country), they had little desire for their children to learn that language or much else about the "old country." Not teaching it to us was their way of leaving their country, that continent, behind. Extolling the virtue of their newly adopted country with its arms open and hope abounding, their gift to this country was us: their children. We would be as American as apple pie, and language was where it started. I accepted that. I never questioned it. Only when I was grown and people asked me if I spoke Hungarian, did I ever stop for one second to think—maybe I should. I did wonder at my total inability to learn other languages throughout my school years as well as my struggle through every language I was ever required to take. I simply concluded I had no facility for language and let it go.

However, when I made a trip to my parents' homeland, Hungary, after their death, I decided it was time for me to make a new attempt to end this language barrier. Mindful of my difficulty with all languages, I scoured the stores for the simplest language tape I could find; you know, the one that indicates that even an idiot can learn a language through these magical tapes—they are still around. I found not one but two sets; I bought them both. I was serious about this enterprise. I listened to each tape over and over and over before my trip. I repeated the words, then the phrases, and concentrated only on the simplest. Still, as soon as I put the tapes away, the words left me, the phrases evaporated into the air. Sometimes, however, here and there, I recognized familiar words, familiar phrases. I recognized them as my father's words and phrases. Mostly, they were the common usage, or as the tapes so nicely put it, the more colloquial way to say the word or phrase. I realized my father had used the same phrases over and over—no surprise, really, when you think about it: Don't many of you, once a phrase is found that seems comfortable, tend to stay with it? Soon, it was a game in which I became interested. It took me back to the times my parents spoke quietly in the evenings, after my sister and I had gone to bed, when I could still hear the soft sounds of their voices, but really didn't know what they were saying—sometimes, though, I admit I got the drift (maybe more by the tone!).

Despite this, I was still listening to those tapes on the long plane trip from Boston to Budapest, thinking, "I will never remember these phrases." When I arrived in Hungary, a magical transformation began to take place: When people spoke to me, with the simple, polite phrases that people use when they meet and greet you in some countries, I surprisingly found myself understanding some of the phrases that were spoken. Doubly wonderful, often the people who spoke to me at the airport, the hotel, and the restaurants supplied me with the very words I needed to respond, straight from my tapes (of course!). As I responded, people smiled. Contact was made. Soon, I began to be slightly less self-conscious—a feeling about language that had plagued me all my life. I started to break a lifelong language barrier. And boy, did I feel smart!

Now I am slowly making my way through French language tapes. French is not really a new language for me. French is the language I took (but never learned to speak) in college, and later in graduate school. But somehow I am, for the very first time in my entire life, very optimistic about learning (or relearning) another language. The motivation is that a little French bistro has opened in this small mountain town where I have a home, and the lovely family (mother, father, two small children) speak French. The wife is bilingual, but speaks French and translates or mixes the words together; the menu, of course, is in French. What a lovely opportunity! She is so pleased when I try the words and phrases out; I am so pleased that my pronunciation seems fine—at least to her. I am beginning to really understand her spoken French, too—a feat I never seemed to be able to master.

This year I had a wonderful surprise reacquainting myself with language. Spending time in bilingual Canada, I find I am able to read the ingredients in supermarkets and descriptions in drug stores in French as well as English—a good thing to be able to do. Sometimes, I don't even realize I am reading one or the other. I know I am working on skills I haven't used for a long while that I have reintroduced myself to. I know it brings a big smile to my face (and why does it seem that more people than usual smile at me too? They seem to!).

Proficiencies, even small ones, aren't to be taken lightly at any stage of life. On such small things, success is measured, confidence restored, and a good feeling about the self sends off signals of satisfaction: feeling smart! A nice experience to have any day.

You could argue, and it is certainly true, that these are not really new learning experiences since I had a basis for both these languages. And I would say yes and remind you that this is a journey to reintroduce or to travel old pathways, long abandoned, and discover new treasures built on the old. That is why they are treasure hunts: You may well have a basis, but the skill has been long put away, in disuse—where you may never have thought much about the possibilities of bringing those rusty skills into the present and using them, expanding them, building on them. That's the point.

Trailblazing

What about you? How many things did you study, but not pursue? How many things have you started to learn and stopped? How many things did you learn, up to a point, but not further—but might still want to learn more about? How many skills do you know are there, but feel they are just out of reach at this point, your skills so rusty?

And what about now? Let's face it, another factor may well have entered into the equation. Like so many of the Silver Generation, you suspect your present stage precludes a renewed or new learning venture. You are hesitant to learn anything new either, even when something flits across your mind, for a moment—even a microsecond—and the thought occurs to you that you might just like to walk that familiar terrain again. So you will need to ask yourself: Does it have to be this way? Do I have to close off my mind to relearning old, still familiar, and once-loved things, or can I, perhaps, build on some foundation that I may still have?

Again, science is on your side: Studies are showing that learning can continue for practically your whole life span, and further, and most important, that previous learning can be accessed. What more do you really need? So in some ways, you might be slower, it may take longer; but in other ways, you may well be wiser, too; you have, after all, a greater knowledge base (and experience!) than those younger than you. Wouldn't this be a good time for you to renew an acquaintance with these old loves and interests?

I urge you to think about this and to jot down some areas of past knowledge, interest, or excitement, some skills and ability level you had reached, things you wanted to pursue and started to—but life got in the way. This would be a good time to consider the possibilities, wouldn't it? Then do it! Do it now—and then continue! (I have inserted a personal survey at the end of this chapter for you.) So start the process of identifying what your goals would be if you could continue some of your past loves, if you could build on your foundation of academic skills as well as experiences and whatever else has gone into the mix that makes up the uniqueness of you.

Learning New Data

So you think you can't learn new material either? You can't absorb information—too much coming down the pike (yes, we are in an age of information overload); too much in areas and disciplines you never heard of; you even find it difficult to contemplate learning more about the areas of expertise you had and expand your knowledge base. The mind just doesn't work that way anymore, you might say. I would dispute that assumption.

I want to share with you the most interesting personal experience I have had recently—doing research for this very book. I believe it illustrates the potential of a successful treasure hunt along old pathways. For research, I used Google's search engine in a way I had not before, for all the reasons you already know: rusty skills and concern about the process—after all, computers are not one of the things we were brought up with, now, are they? My grandson had made it remarkably easy, though; my husband, not a computer whiz himself, for the same reasons, gave me a quick tip: Put your search in here, just the words; don't worry about more.

And so, I started to research some of the concepts used in this paper: short- and long-term memory, for example. So much appeared, a lot of it technical. I started to move through the material, slowly at first, but then more rapidly, then even faster ... I started to print out pertinent material, too. Before I knew it, I realized that my reading speed, which had always been excellent, but had lain somewhat dormant, was operating in full gear: reading, associating, selecting, deciding; it was a heady experience. As the papers came out of the printer, I was circling the pertinent parts—I had already read and understood enough to know which parts I wanted to underline, to use further, to better understand. At the end of the sessions, I knew I had read, absorbed, and saved a large number of important papers. It wasn't the amount I printed, that had already been selected; it was the amount I read through, skimmed through, surveyed, understood so quickly. So much for not being able to absorb new data, or for being able to absorb it relatively quickly, integrate it, and utilize it! I couldn't believe how much I had absorbed; how many of my purely academic skills were available to me still for the using. How many different knowledge bases I had perused; how easy it was for me to select sources of integrity. I even found fine sources that allowed me to e-mail intelligent questions about the subject and received responses that were extremely helpful. A whole field opened to me; a whole new window on the world.

And I found myself saying hogwash (again), so much for the mind slowing down, shutting down, simply not being able to learn or learn quickly. That concept should be broken into fragments and dumped into the nearest trash can. Yes, I was surprised to think that I had bought into that one too—this awareness of the potential of those entering that age, those of the Silver Generation, I realized will have to be a continuum, and many formerly accepted attitudes needed to be tested under many circumstances. I vowed to myself before I buy into one of those attitudes again, I will test, test, and test again. I truly believe that is sound advice.

I want to add that science is also finding evidence to support the ability to continue learning. Science is also disputing these contradictory assumptions. A friend sent me an article from *Scientific American* entitled "Saving New Brain Cells." There was much in that article to lend credence to the ability of the brain to learn new things; not only learning, but making that effort to learn will help to preserve "newly minted nerve cells." Further, there appear to be new neurons involved with new learning—and it is suggested if we want to keep our brains in shape, it would not hurt to learn something new. Consider the ramifications for those entering that age. I don't have to take you to that garbage pail, now, do I?

Exploring Another Hidden Treasure Within (Muscle Memory)

What follows is another of the treasure hunts I have made in recent years: Different from, but arguably as powerful as, the rediscovery of language, was the discovery I could relearn difficult piano pieces that I dearly loved. As a child, I took seven years of piano lessons and then stopped. I wanted to continue; I had a plan to review all the music I had learned and perfected—well, never quite perfected, that was the problem. It seemed to me I rarely reached a point of playing a piece through without a mistake, before I left it and went on to something brand new—more demanding. Sometimes, though, I had moments of such emotional expressiveness and felt I was being true to the great composer's work. Those were special moments when my joy momentarily knew no bounds. But leaving them too quickly to go on to some other piece, I felt I lost the level of accomplishment I wanted to attain. My piano teacher, Bernice, whom I loved, was sad when I stopped taking lessons, but I think we both knew I was never going to be a concert pianist (I was too shy!), I was never even going to play in a school band or orchestra either, for the same reason. So I stopped. But I was going to continue—or so I thought—playing for myself. I really did intend to go back to and memorize some great composers I had learned, as well as some smaller but no less beautiful pieces of Chopin and Schumann that I loved, BUT I DIDN'T. Those were busy years— teenage years—and well, so many things intruded. Then I was into engagement and marriage and family and home and work, so those pages of music discolored into that parchment color and frazzled a bit. But I never let go of the pieces of music I had loved so.

Decades later, children grown, work reduced, I found myself staring at a piano my husband and I had inherited from his parents and stored in friends' homes for many decades. We finally brought the piano to the mountain house we had bought; we had it fixed and tuned—there it was, finally truly in our possession once again. The thought occurred to me that I had the time to play that piano now. After all those years; the excitement began to build. I literally dug out my music from under stacks of other things saved. I sat down to play. I would like to tell you how great I was, how the fingers flew over the keyboard, how all the skills I had were still there, hadn't wasted away—but I can't.

What I can tell you is an interesting tale of a different type of treasure hunt—not any less exciting. As I pulled out my tattered and torn pages and started to work through the melody notes with my right hand, I heard refrains of yesteryear. But when I started to join right hand to the left, it was not only that I was rusty, but that I could no longer read some of the notes that were in the lower bass or higher treble clefs. (Maybe I had never really learned them well enough.) I was disappointed, very disappointed, but I persevered. After all, failure was not unknown to me throughout my life; it was always a possibility in many things I had done. So I continued on: My reading skills improved a bit, and my fingers moved more skillfully and confidently. Finally, one day I began to feel, once again, some of the magic of the music through my fingers. Those hard notes, those high and low octave chords, were still not within my ability to sight read, but the magic was still there. I could have gotten an instructor to help me brush up, I suppose, but I was determined. (Or I simply didn't think of it.) I agonized trying to work it out. Over and over, I played that first part of the *Hungarian*

Rhapsody and that Chopin étude. I felt obsessed. I would find myself playing the notes over and over in my head as I drifted off to sleep.

One day, I was playing better, but knew I still had miles to go, when I became stuck over some chords. Frustrated, I looked away for a moment. I remember it was snowing. Looking out on the giant trees beginning to wear a coat of white, it was not very difficult for my mind to drift off, caught up in the movement of the snowflakes. When I returned from this reverie, to my great surprise and infinite joy, my hands suddenly seemed to remember what to do! They wandered around the piano keys mindlessly. They seemed to have a mind of their own from a life I had lived a long time ago, when the magical treasure of music was mine. My hands continued to wander over the keys. Suddenly, my hands were playing the correct chords—the ones I hadn't been able to remember and struggled to see on the page—while my right and left hands were synchronizing! My heart seemed to skip a beat. Was it possible? Of course it was: Scientists would have a ready explanation. I'm sure they would say something about the power of muscle memory and would elaborate as to how it was able to take over. Yes, we would nod and say yes, that of course makes sense and we understand that muscle memory can, of course, do this. But as my hands flew over the chords without me, at least without the conscious effort that had been such a strain, it was a fantastic experience. For me, it was a breakthrough, a way back to that moment in time when I had found something I loved and left it, a treasure hunt down a path of such joy and satisfaction.

Postscript

I cannot say I was suddenly magnificent and that it is still not work to move through a new or old piece … but it is something I love, something I love for me, something I am mastering for my own pleasure and enjoyment and that of a few people I can selectively allow into my private select space. The experience has also given me confidence that a part of me remembers and is more ready to receive treasures that may be waiting for me. Hunting for hidden treasure within me that can be restored to me has become an exciting and heady experience.

Do I play all the time? No! Do I practice a lot? In spurts! But I have periods during which I use the muscle memory technique and know those difficult passages will come—and I have relearned by heart some of the magnificent pieces of my childhood. I have a little Chopin étude I can play by heart, and of course *Für Elise* has not abandoned me, nor for the most part the *Hungarian Rhapsody*—although some of those chords are a stretch for fragile fingers so I change the chords a bit. What I have gained from this experience is confidence and direction. I find myself looking forward to perhaps other treasures that may lie in wait for me—dormant, perhaps, but not lost. Such potentially rich treasures lying in wait in my personal treasure chest makes my future more exciting to contemplate.

Since then, I have gone on other treasure hunts within the self: picked up on other things that were on my list of things I started, wanted to pursue, but didn't. And I have made my list of other things too. Perhaps it is time for you to do that, if you haven't already. Pick from your personal list. If you have not made one, now is the time to do it—and prioritize. IF NOT NOW, WHEN?

Sharing Your Treasures

Remember to make use of your newly discovered treasures, those you want to share. In view of what we are discussing, there are multiple outcomes of sharing: pleasure, pride, confidence, feeling good about yourself—and feeling smart. You will want to bring in those lines of poetry you may have memorized and expand your horizons as well as those of the people around you. People may just surprise you as they pull out those long stored, but never forgotten, bits of poetry and great lines from Shakespeare—or even Ogden Nash. Many people carry around far more than they think to share, but are quite willing, actually pleased, to have an environment to share these treasures. And don't strain too hard to find the exact right moment. Chances are you, as I, have had practice in the art of conversation—even if you need to stretch to reach your subject, even if it seems a non sequitur, perhaps? What do you have to lose? (You might want to keep this story in mind: My husband got carried away one day in a law class, he is fond of relating, and went on and on about a subject of law he was interested in, but turned out to be unrelated to the legal discussion of the day. Nonetheless, the erudite professor did not interrupt him. After the monologue—in which the class seemed quite interested—the professor said gently, "A brilliant response, but every once in a while, a professor has a right to ask, what brings forth these comments?" An example of both good manners and the right to get to a point you are interested in and passionate about in a discussion. Surely if it could be done in this circumstance, it can be done in a social setting.)

You can also bring all sorts of interesting literary and other tidbits into your conversations: Moby Dick was a white whale. Did you remember that? And the significance? Or if you live near places like Bedford, Massachusetts, where you can still see signs of the old whaling industry, which Melville spends about a hundred pages on, plan an outing. Whatever part of the country you live in, scenes from great books often took root and great people lived there. So much to think about and include in conversations, don't you think? Whatever your interest, mine happens to be obvious, but yours may be science, technology, biology, medicine; the world is being made over: All are

145

unique and fascinating areas alive with possibilities—your treasures for living your life exactly as you want.

So bring your gifts with you and share them: A friend of mine is incredibly talented and remembers so many refrains of songs, complete scores from Gilbert and Sullivan and those wonderful Broadway musicals of the sixties as well, which his parents played over and over again when he was a boy. Into so many conversations about life, issues, and politics come those beautifully apt refrains as good and as fascinatingly placed as Shakespeare.

I attended another concert recently, and there the two old friends, James Levine of the Boston Symphony Orchestra, sitting on a bench with Daniel Barenboim, were doing a duet for four hands. As I watched these two old friends, the refrains of Simon and Garfunkel passed through my mind: "Old friends, old friends ... sat on a park bench like bookends ... when did we get to be seventy?" Oh, yes, I found that applicable. I have been telling people about this wonderful musical event, sharing it, both the experience and my personal reaction. Isn't that what embellishes life? I think it does. I'll bet that one is repeated because, of course, my generation, yours, and many to come—with the help of huge concerts in Woodstock or Foxboro Stadium or Central Park—have kept alive the magical music of these two wonderful people, Simon and Garfunkel. And by the way, how did they know what it would be like to be seventy? I ask that question a lot these days. Their words ring so true for me!

But for those of this Silver Generation, perhaps those old friends will do more than sit on a park bench: Perhaps they will be relaxing after a game of tennis, or horseback riding (they closed the last stable in Manhattan, didn't they?), or fast-walking around the reservoir path, or—the possibilities are endless. And they are within the grasp of this

Silver Generation, your generation, for those of you who are willing to reach far enough—to reach for the silver (and glittery) lining.

Concluding Remarks

Once you start to treasure hunt, to tap into this rich resource within yourself, I predict a feeling of euphoria will embrace you. You will be on your way to tapping into hidden treasures that are unique to you—and never want to stop drawing from your newfound storehouse of treasures. Use this newly restored knowledge! Use it for all of your days. Use it for every occasion! Use it as a basis of conversation. Use it in a slow, deliberate, triumphant way—and let no one deny you the privilege; it is, in fact, your right. This is the foundation for the rest of your life. Build on it with pride, bring the data with you as a gift, and bring it into your daily life often: use the experience in social settings; as an entrance into more serious conversations; or even in letters—if that beautiful art is still available to you. (You might want to try to initiate letter writing with a dear friend who has moved.) The point is to hunt for these treasures on an almost daily basis, if you can, and to share them abundantly: They are you and they are a gift to you and from you, and for others who share your life. Don't minimize your sophisticated skills and knowledge base gained over a lifetime.

I leave you with this story from a dear friend with whom I spent many years of professional life. He would always say each of is a unique individual; we each have our own strengths; but more, we each have our own beauty; our goodness; our unique perspective. No one is quite like any other, he would say—and I knew he meant it. I have carried those simple but eloquent words with me through the years, and they have often given my heart a lift. At different times, it has meant different things. Now it seems to mean that uniqueness is also a responsibility to live life and participate in life as fully as possible.

What I take away from this is what my friend just added as I exchanged e-mails with him: "Every human," he said, "is unique with a unique set of experiences determined by time and space." That uniqueness is your gift to yourself—and to others.

PERSONAL SURVEY

List my strengths.[10] What skills, abilities, and knowledge bases do I have?

What areas of interest did I have that I intended to pursue but didn't, or started and stopped, but meant to continue?

What skills and knowledge bases do I have in part or whole that I have not used for years?

What knowledge or skill or ability did I intend to pursue but didn't pursue?

---

10 Weaknesses are not being dealt with here; we are ignoring them: They don't matter, unless they are areas of everyday necessities, and then they do matter to the extent that you do not compensate for them or use some technique, in part, to deal with them. Regarding other weaknesses, my advice is to ignore them, live with them, accept them, and forget them: We cannot be perfect.

What might still interest me? If I pursue these areas, how can I utilize them in my life now?

What impediments are there for me to pursue them? How can I get past these hurdles?

Chapter 11

YOUR PERSONAL RETRIEVAL SYSTEM

A Theory

For those of you in this new generation, getting in touch with your own Personal Retrieval System (PRS)—that is the knowledge base within: the sum total of all you have learned and all you have experienced (or much of it); in other words, your own storage chest within the self—is not as difficult or daunting a task as you might think: You need to understand the concept of this remarkable data base of personally stored knowledge and explore it; you need to discover your long-term memory is working for you, and you need to have the confidence in yourself that you can access, retrieve and, yes, utilize this vast source of personal knowledge you have within yourself for new adventures as you enter this marvelous age of great potential. Once you start, and you feel the exhilaration and empowerment, you dear members of the Silver Generation will never be the same. Let the Silver Generation begin.

This chapter will allow you to become further acquainted and comfortable with, challenged by, and tantalized by the limitless possibilities contained in your Personal Retrieval System. When this brand-new twenty-first century is looked back on from its end point (as the telephone expanded communication and as trains expanded boundaries for the last century, which affected every facet of life), I believe it will be, without a doubt, the computer plus Internet access and its ever-broadening arsenal of magical possibilities that will be the hallmarks of radical changes in the twenty-first century.

Some generations are given great gifts: From time immemorial, humankind has found magical gifts or imagined them. In fairy tales, there was the power of magic; in pagan days, the "thunderbolt of Zeus" was looked at with awe as a source of great magical power (although many of you will agree, the gift of fire from Prometheus was the greater magical gift to humankind). When the wheel was invented, humankind no longer had to use feet or oxen to travel, the world became smaller, and humankind could travel and move and find what was needed to survive. When Moses came down from the mountain with ten short magical phrases written on stone tablets that would serve somehow to establish the beginning of civilization as we know it, who can deny the magical elements operating there? (Anyone who has second thoughts should see *The Ten Commandments*, the classic movie with Charlton Heston, fully bearded, the white of his hair giving a glimpse of wisdom and grandeur as he thunders down that mountain with the tablets.)

And who can say that Edison's electric light was not magic as light came to humankind through the wonders of a bulb? Before that, for so long people had to carry a torch with fire from one place to another for fear they would not be able to make fire again and that their world would turn back to darkness—certainly the torch was magic. Today, we still commemorate this magic, as every four years a torch is carefully lit from the eternal fire and carried over land by strong runners who pass the torch from one to another over land and sea, until it can be delivered to the site of the present-day Olympics, by which humankind shows its reverence for that magical moment—and then the games begin: a tribute to strength and durability, achievement, and perpetuity.

Certainly the torch had, and continues to have, a strong quality of magic for all people. And then the telephone—the magic thing people screamed into, not believing that the voice could be carried so far over the magic wires (telephone wires), and so it has gone.

I have no doubt that for this generation, the computer and all its manifestations will stand out and hold its own as the magical wand that brought and shall bring manifold untold gifts not yet even dreamed of—perhaps more changes than the sum total of all of the previous changes since the beginning of humankind. So it is only right that this dynamic Silver Generation—who, after all, developed the computer and the Internet—should be the recipients on the threshold of what some are calling the greatest medical and scientific benefits in history: massive increases in longevity and health, and untold, never-before-known riches. They will benefit from cell regeneration for aging minds as well as replacement parts for their aging bodies, and they will be privy to further untold miracles. Remarkably and appropriately enough, too, the Silver Generation may already well have magic powers of its own, emanating from a personal source within the brain that can be more readily accessible than previously thought and used another day. I have called this potential magic your Personal Retrieval System—your own personal computer within your brain.

I believe within your own lifetime lies the unique opportunity to access this highly personal, highly specialized Personal Retrieval System. Being granted longevity and health; coupled with the fortunate way in which you were educated, will allow you to partake of the wonderful gifts of the twenty-first century. Think of the power and wonder and glory of harnessing your own data base that can access past knowledge for you. Who is more deserving of magic of your own making than this dynamic, educated, deeply probing, and able Silver Generation?

Ah, what wonders may await us. This Silver Generation may come of age yet!

Understanding Your Personal Retrieval System

You may not have stopped to reflect on the fact that you, my dear peers and members of the Silver Generation, have a Personal Retrieval System not unlike a computer within your own brain—one that you not only can access, but upon which you can also build. Wouldn't this be a personal gift of manna from heaven—another magic wand to the twenty-first century? Like a computer, your Personal Retrieval System contains vast amounts of data stored in long-term memory banks, capable of sorting, making associations, and selecting, and, so important to the Silver Generation, capable of perpetual retrieval. That means you should be able to access it, actually, throughout most of your lifetime. The more you have learned, and learned well, the greater your potential for accessing and retrieving knowledge within the self. The potential for reaching a knowledge base that is the sum total of all your learning and experience is almost mind- boggling. Think of the power and wonder and glory of harnessing that data base within the self—past knowledge, stored away, capable of retrieval at your command in your brain: that's brainpower!

Although I'm sure many of you already access this storehouse of knowledge, you probably have not given thought to its powerful potential or your ability to make it work for you. If you are like so many of your peers, you are happy enough when some past information pops into your head and not really surprised when you can't quickly remember a piece of information. But think of the potential of building a bridge to your PRS. Think of the possibilities of harnessing this power source on an ongoing basis for the rest of your life and making it really work for you.

Your longer life span heralds the continued absorption, storage, and retrieval of an enormous data base more like the Renaissance model that is still much admired. Think Michelangelo, Rembrandt, Newton, and the magic of that time we so admire when people seemed to absorb so much knowledge and be successful in so many fields over a life span. With the life expectancy being extended, the Silver Generation may have the time, over the anticipated extra span of life, to duplicate that magnificent period of learning and creating. Only few people have done so since that remarkable time. Ben Franklin, scientist, inventor, statesman, scholar, seemed one of our rare examples of a Renaissance man. There are others, of course, but I think you will agree, it is not a commonplace phenomenon. Given the gifts that are on the horizon, the possibilities for this Silver Generation seem endless. What an exciting time to be living.

Applying the New Paradigm

This newly developing theory that advocates using brain cells or possibly losing them has an interesting and important bearing on the treasure hunts and accessing of your Personal Retrieval System, which has been at the heart of Part II of this book—discovering and using your strengths within your mind. The major thrust here has been to look back to the foundations of personal knowledge, skills, and interests you have gained throughout your life and build on them. In this way, not only will you be utilizing your brainpower—the knowledge base you already have—but you will have the opportunity to expand and extend that base wherever you choose to take it. Regardless of what you do with it, there is no doubt you will be using your brain in all of its infinite capabilities—some of which, I am sure that neither you nor science are as yet aware of—all the magnificent possibilities existing there. But by this time, you already have begun to realize, if you had not before, that your generation will be pathfinders and trailblazers. With the addition of this newest gift as well, those entering that age may well reap multiple rewards.

Again, an analogy to a computer seems appropriate: I strongly believe that you have a rich retrieval system within the self. You have been storing data all your life: Remember those exercises in learning, testing, relearning that were a prime pedagogical technique of our schooling system I discussed earlier? Remember the theory behind them: If you learn, get tested, relearn ad nauseam ... well, maybe you never quite thought of this application of that knowledge base to your silver years? But that learning was promulgated on the premise that you would keep on acquiring more of the basic data, and further, that you could and would be able to draw upon it in your later years, in your professional years, and in your ... how about NOW?!

So you thought the computer was a new development that had absolutely no relation to you: think again. Systems are made in the image of humans and their acute powers of observation. I am not being flippant: Look up at an airplane; do you think it was designed to look like a bird out of a whim or because the avionics of flight are built upon an observable flying object? And what about the first nuclear-powered submarine being named the *Nautilus*: Did you think it was a coincidence that the wonderful early science fiction book by Jules Verne, *Twenty Thousand Leagues Under the Sea* also had a submarine named *Nautilus*? We know when to borrow a good idea, especially when the underpinnings are beginning to be rather solid, sound, and scientific—after all, it is called *science* fiction for a reason. So the name, Nautilus, was borrowed from that fascinating science fiction story—which was only right, don't you think?

This is the moment for members of the dynamic Silver Generation to draw on that vast arsenal of stored data, which was so kindly input into your very own Personal Retrieval System: your brain. Wouldn't it be a supreme irony (poetic irony, of course) if those early educational processes that you endured largely because you had no choice, when you were inundated with the repetitiveness of it all, at one level can now serve you?! Think about it! I think the possibilities are exciting: Wasn't the concept that we would eventually get it ... store it ... and retrieve it as we needed it? There was no time limitation built into the retrieval of information in that pedagogical learning system that most of you were submitted to, now, was there?

So I ask you to think back once again to the time when you were in that mode of taking everything in, each day, every day, and all day, and how much extra attention you paid to those special areas that were your personal interest areas because you liked them, because you enjoyed playing with the ideas, because they fascinated you? And think that you are likely to have them at your disposal! For myself, it was literature; perhaps for you, science. For me, Jane Austen, George Eliot, Dickens, and later, Dostoevsky (mostly all of his novels); in poetry, the wonderful (but poignant and illuminating) Romantics: Wordsworth, Shelly, Byron, and Keats; later, the troublesome T. S. Eliot and the ever-faithful, always dear Robert Frost, who captured my heart and mind. Entire subject areas of interest to me that I gathered bits and pieces of, whenever I could, but certainly had no extensive time to pursue, were Greek and Roman mythology, and later, an offshoot of that, the myths of the goddesses, as well as an endless fascination with creation, the Old Testament aspect, the creation myths, and later science—leaving me with an endless fascination of the interrelationship between them. Needless to say, so much of that has not been well enough explored by me, but of course still provides endless interest, musings. Added to that, Camus's intriguing thought in *Sisyphus*: So science ends in a metaphor, still running through my mind—too much for a lifetime? Maybe and maybe not!

And what was it you loved? And wouldn't you rather spend your time thinking and talking about rediscovered areas of interest than trying to remember what you had for breakfast or whether this is Tuesday or Wednesday, so you could get an "A" in someone else's checklist of characteristics that indicate that you are or are not losing it? *Reductio ad absurdum.* For those of you in this new generation, getting in touch with your own Personal Retrieval System (read: brainpower) seems no longer as difficult or daunting a task as you might think. You need to explore this avenue of potential knowledge base; you need to discover your long-term memory is working for you; and you need to have confidence in yourself, which you will gain by discovering these treasures. Not really a Catch-22, because once you start and have a little success, confidence will be a concomitant result, as will exhilaration and the feeling of empowerment.

Discovering Your Personal Retrieval System

To have at your fingertips this monumental gift, what a challenge, what excitement, and what possibilities! I feel it is like opening a hidden door no different than the fairy tale when Beauty, in a *Beauty and the Beast on Ice* version I saw, unlocks the treasure behind the door in the castle: she finds to her heart's delight a massive library lined literally from floor to ceiling with books!

By now you are wondering how you go about discovering your Personal Retrieval System. What is the formula? How do you start? You will need quiet time to think, to remember, to pontificate, to become aware; in other words, a consciousness raising and an awakening of the self. In short, you will simply need the time, quiet, and application of yourself perhaps to some past substantive project in which you had great interest, did substantial work, thought or spoke about frequently—maybe produced a paper—or in some way utilized material that was primarily interesting to you. In these circumstances, because of your deep and abiding interest, your Personal Retrieval System was most probably in operation; in other words, you saved it in the long-term memory banks of your brain! Once you start to do this on a regular basis, once you start the process, you will enable yourself to move into fast gear as you reach within yourself for potentially the richest treasure of all.

Accessing your PRS can best be understood at this point by relating one person's realization of this potent ability in the self. I offer you these personal examples, then, because I believe they are the shortest route to understanding the process of accessing your own knowledge base and retrieving the data. You may only be limited by your interest, your curiosity, your motivation, and your perseverance. Given the nature of this extraordinary journey within the self, I believe it cannot be other than a truly exciting and exhilarating journey.

One Person's Journey

Writing used to be such a chore for me: A love-hate relationship existed for such a long time. I loved writing; I hated the constant frustration while I searched for the perfect word. I hated it more when I couldn't remember the poet's name, or the quote I wanted was on the tip of my tongue, yet eons away, or when the same thing happened with books I had read and novelists I had studied in depth, and whose complete works I had read. What time-consuming searches I had to do (this was pre-computer search engines, if one can think that there was such a time, pre-Yahoo, or Google, or Wikipedia). However, the point is, I struggled, and the process interrupted the creative writing process.

As the years went by—and I read, and I read—I became more proficient in my own areas of expertise and could access those things that I was working on with relative ease. Of course I thought it was due to my present working knowledge base that enabled me to more readily remember many quotes and forego the arduous task of the looking-up process—or have to stop the creative part—to get a broader knowledge base. I didn't think beyond that; if anything, I simply thought— hoped—I had simply become smart, smug, and satisfied. Or I thought that I had reviewed sufficiently for this project to remind myself of all the material I needed on hand as well as the newer material added on from current sources for this particular project. If anything occurred to me about the process I was utilizing, it was probably annoyance with myself for not remembering more, but I don't remember more than a moment of time spent on that thought, before I let it go: That was the way life was, after all. Or so I then thought.

I do remember one experience that stood out for me: One summer in the seventies, I took a summer school course with a professor from Oxford. She was teaching Victorian literature: I chose a topic related to early women writers like George Eliot and Jane Austen for my term paper. I wished to explore the question of whether these writers were early feminists or cop-out artists. I thought it appropriate at the time. I loved these women writers; they had shaped my early life and remained a part of me. I had studied them, written about them, and measured myself against them. I was taking this course a few decades later to renew my acquaintance with them, take the opportunity to reread some works, and go further in my study. For the specific assignment, I reread some of their books and tackled the term paper. I remember writing the paper in a few sittings: no look-ups, no outside research, no reams of secondary sources—just myself and the primary material. I wrote with hardly a pause. After the paper was written, I went to the library for the obligatory secondary sources and apt quotations to strengthen my paper. I remember all this, not because the mark I got was A-minus, but because the comment was "A fine paper, but you relied too heavily on outside sources." Further, there was an additional comment suggesting that if I had been able to distance myself from the secondary sources, the result would have been more creative and satisfying (which I took to mean I would have earned a straight A).

I gave a great deal of thought to that heavy reliance on outside sources noted! Well, I didn't doubt the esteemed professor or her capable and knowledgeable assistant instructor, but I never ceased wondering exactly how I could have relied on and emulated the thoughts and discussions of secondary sources when I read them only after I wrote the paper and simply pulled out appropriate quotes that fit my material? Now I think differently: I think perhaps the information I used was from former study, reading, thinking, and the information came more from my personal data bank: my brain, which I had accessed (past data recorded) and unknowingly retrieved. A far more sensible explanation for the comments made on my paper. How else to explain it? I am sure many of you have had the same type of experience.

So it would seem to me that when you are thinking of doing a project or merely thinking about a serious subject, you might just want to find the time, the place, and the quiet to begin to become conscious of the stored data you already possess and might be able to access first, before you go to outside sources. (And that goes for those times you say to yourself: "Oh, I knew that at one time, but ...") The process is not rocket science; it is simply a process, which once uncovered, can yield rich treasures for you—especially as you enter that age. It may also help enormously to offset those doubts about what you may be losing (like knowing what day it is!), and replace those doubts with the enormous satisfaction of what you are gaining.

More recently, while working on a large academic project after many years away from the subject matter, I became aware that something else was definitely happening. As I wrote away, I was more aware of the library of my mind. By this time, I was becoming confident that material being brought to bear on my present themes, thoughts, and values were from past memory stored. In other words, my present studies were continuing from and building on past ones—many from a surprisingly long time ago. When I started to fill in full quotations and names of authors, poets, poems, and philosophers from time periods of antiquity that I had not thought about for years—and other information that came from data sources not touched upon for years (try decades)—I finally understood that what was working was my PRS: a vast arsenal of data stored, learned years and decades ago, at my fingertips, different from and in addition to the current material I was reading and studying. That is when I thought with great astonishment—and then enjoyment and excitement (an epiphany: thank you, Mr. Joyce)—that I was truly accessing my own Personal Retrieval System in my brain. In fact, I was accessing and retrieving material learned in the past—sometimes, from more decades ago than I would readily admit.

As you would suspect, I found a vast storehouse of information was on subjects I had loved and lingered over: subjects I am still immensely interested in, subjects I now write about or plan to write about in detail. Having developed the confidence in this process working for me, I was able to move into full gear. Recently, a colleague and I got together to discuss the lack of leadership evident in the world today: a very "now" subject. He is a business/management/educator type, and I am the opposite: literature and the law, but we are both seriously interested in educating leaders for tomorrow—tomorrow fast becoming today, sooner than we thought. Together, we thought through a concept that has started to be utilized, but we had our individual thrusts. The audience would be those who were already making their way in the world, but not yet prepared for global leadership. We thought it would be rewarding to join together leadership theories and classical literature. Not an original idea, but we believe that by drawing on the ideas and events of yesterday to expand their focus, combined with understanding the broader philosophy of leadership and the global needs of leadership today, we would address a special application to leadership needs of today in an interesting way. So "Leadership Training Through Classical Literature" was developed. There was a lot of renewing of classical literature to find the appropriate examples, to read, reread, and draw on knowledge learned so long ago, while at the same time utilizing leadership theories of today to move into a broader, higher principled, and practical application to today's vast challenges.

Much research and reading were necessary: linking the great leaders and thinkers, the philosophers and statesmen, the writers who understood greatness and the fall of greatness—all this had to come together. As I moved along with this project, there was much struggle, but much joy. The treasures I found (yes, within the self), the knowledge base I had (within the self), and the expansion of that knowledge base as I built on what I had known and moved onto what I had wanted to know, but left to another time— another treasure hunt, which turned out to be an exhilarating experience. And it has worked! Hopefully, the material will soon be published, but more importantly, a testament to that success after I have entered that age.

So think about what happened in the above chain of events. Even with Google and Yahoo at my fingertips, I still gain an immense pleasure from the quote, the phrase, the author popping right into my head at the moment I need her or him—and I do not have to stop to find the material. (And no interruption in my creative thought process!) Just the delightful exhilaration of being able to extract the pertinent information I desire from my PRS. I have gained a great deal of trust and confidence in acknowledging, accessing, retrieving, and building on this base, too. I strongly believe this is available to all of those entering that age; I believe it to be the greatest gift we can give ourselves—and I truly believe, if the interest is there, the treasure can be found: a Personal Retrieval System within the self. Every day, I remember more (yes, I remember more of what is exciting to me, my knowledge base, my thoughts, my life pursuits), and I am able to access and retrieve and continue to gain the confidence to let it happen.

Accessing Your Personal Retrieval System: Are You Ready?

I believe you already have the tools needed to access your Personal Retrieval System. Further, with consciousness, willpower, and understanding your achievements over your lifetime, you are more than prepared to move forward. Once you initiate your conscious thought process, you will be ready to proceed at your own pace, and once you move ahead with accessing and retrieving from your PRS, no one but yourself can stop you. Yours is a generation not to be toyed with. You have much more living to do and, for some, much to achieve. I expect that many of you have already started, but not quite thought of the power of the brain harnessed as a potent PRS: Now, hopefully, you will begin or expand your journey.

SOME BASIC RULES FOR SUCCESS

The basic rules are simple, far simpler than you would have thought:

- Know you have a store of information in your Personal Retrieval System, mainly within your long-term memory bank.

- When you have that moment where you are talking or writing or thinking and suddenly you have a vague recollection of the material you are seeking (whether it is a fact, a piece of data, a name, an event, a period of history, a phrase, a philosopher or philosophy, a concept, a value, a time, or anything else your mind has focused on), stay with it!

- Let it come! Don't say, "Darn, I used to know that, but I can't think of it now"; it may not, in fact, be lost knowledge; don't moan over the fact that you can't recall it; don't beat up on yourself about all the learning you had, all the studying you did, all the research and writing, and now you can't even remember the heart of it. Stay with it ... chances are that it will come to you in a shorter time than you might imagine.

- Let your mind work on it in its own way. This is the most important facet. Stay calm, stay focused; see what unfolds. Many times, it will come to you momentarily: pop into your mind when you least expect; it may not be that moment (but oftentimes it is); it may not even be that day (but oftentimes it is); it may take a while (but so what?!). The more open you are; the more relaxed; the more confident that you may well be able to reach that richness within, the more probable it is that you will.

Once you start accessing the wealth within your PRS, you will never be the same. Trust it, test it, access it, and use it. And for those of you who have been nodding as you read this, thinking to yourself, "Of course this happens," you are already on your way. Let it happen more; expect it to happen more often: embrace it; understand what is happening—and develop that ready link to your very own Personal Retrieval System.

Concluding Remarks

Your Personal Retrieval System is a whole new dynamic, and as you pay closer attention to some of the responses you give offhand or answers and information that come to you in the strangest way, you will start to realize that a) you already access this Personal Retrieval System without having realized it; b) you merely hadn't identified it or given it the credit it deserves; and c) you may well have started to access or retrieve it, but not to the extent to which you are able. Once you realize the possibilities, you will have entered upon one of the most exhilarating journeys of your life.

There is the opportunity for this dynamic Silver Generation to be in the forefront of a revolutionary, exciting arena of mental development of limitless potential. By having the ability to reach your long-term memory bank where you stored so much—similar to a computer, as discussed earlier, that emulates, simulates, and copies the human brain—by expanding these facets within your brain (by using and accessing them), you will be at a tremendous advantage: You will jump-start a process just now being researched and far-reaching in its implications.

The power of the brain is just beginning to be understood, and it promises to uncover much that will be of rich use to the Silver Generation. Already, research has shown that long-term memory banks hold rich promise of more accessibility; that long-term memory may well be drawn on for more useful, more personally significant data; and that it may offer, indeed, a pathway to resources stored over a lifetime that can be harnessed. Imagine a personal data base of stored knowledge from which you can access and retrieve long-term information that is of interest and excitement to you. What a magical gift to the Silver Generation—to you! What marvelous discoveries in science and medicine of the capacity and use of the human brain this century promises.

Chapter 12

EMPOWERING THE SILVER GENERATION

Aging Defiantly

Empowerment is what this book is really about: the empowerment of those entering that age at the most amazing life-extending period in the history of the world; empowerment to make the world work for you; empowerment to live your life as you choose; empowerment to carve and sculpt and reinforce and risk and enjoy life; and empowerment to enable you to live with dignity and integrity and make the powerful contribution you may want and can give the world in which you live—because you have spectacular potential within and are being given enormous gifts of longevity and health, sometimes seemingly magical gifts from outside: Use these wisely, use them well, but use them!

Empowerment is another way of taking charge of the situations that face those entering that age. It is the awareness that rights that you have (or should have) are being impeded or trampled upon. It is the decision that those who would deprive you of your rights, whether to a hospitable social environment or to understanding and support from family and friends, are simply wrong, and you will need to recognize that these attitudes and behavior are inappropriate. Empowerment is the moment that you truly decide this is not acceptable and say, "I will not allow it." It is the moment you assert, "I will do what I must to ensure that the behavior toward me as well as the social environment are both supportive and positive." It is that moment you decide, "I will do whatever it takes to ensure that I am not pushed aside, treated unfairly or disrespectfully, or made to feel I am being prepared to be put out to pasture." It is the moment you know you can, and think and feel, "I will not allow a lifetime of knowledge, experience, and ability to go to waste!" In other words, it is that moment when you say, "Stop the world!" And truly decide, "From now on, we're gonna do things my way," that you are empowered. It is also what I have referred to as aging defiantly!

Empowerment is what this book is really about: empowerment of those entering that age at the most amazing life-extending period in the history of the world; empowerment that will allow you to make the world work for you; empowerment to live your life as you choose—and take full advantage of the opportunities before you; and empowerment to carve and sculpt and reinforce and risk and enjoy life. Empowerment is also the confidence to know you can still contribute to the world in which you live—because you have spectacular potential within and also you are being given a strong ally in science and medicine. If this new generation of robust and intelligent, highly skilled individuals, moving into their senior years (but not their vegetative ones), is to succeed in the achievements that have been posed throughout this book, then the outmoded barriers and hurdles that stand in their way must be met head on, as they age with dignity, integrity, and spunk—and yes, as they age defiantly.

Now, readers, you didn't expect to get to the end of the book without that defiance aspect of aging coming into play, did you? There is one last inappropriate behavior pattern that must be dealt with now that you have reached this point in the book. This behavior pattern of intimidation seems to abound in our society. (Is it that it has become more acceptable as manners have declined and aggressive behavior has come to dominate many of our social environments? You need only to look at some of the purported TV news stations, to see people screaming at each other, interrupting each other, and asking—with smirks—questions that seem intended to belittle and intimidate.) Regardless, I would be remiss in not addressing and dealing with this potentially great ego-distressing social behavior pattern … and so it is presented here. Although there are many strategies and techniques that I will discuss in the chapter that follows on intimidation management for warding off the pains and penalties of intimidation, I must say at the outset that the most effective technique is often defiance. Like it or not, spunk, along with aging defiantly, may be the most effective technique to overcome the hindrance to the Silver Generation's pursuit of certain aspects of their dynamic new world. There are variations and gradations of this theme, as you will discover as you move through these chapters.

You could wait for society to change its attitudes and behavior patterns. Society will certainly change, eventually, true. But at this moment, when science and medicine are outstripping the practices of society toward the Silver Generation, racing headlong into creation of fantastic opportunities for the future that will enable the Silver Generation, your generation, to live full and productive lives far beyond any expectations dreamed of in the past, the question becomes, Are you willing to wait? What will you be missing out on if you allow yourself to obsess over societal attitudes and societal behaviors toward you, like social intimidation? How long will it take? Don't you have more important things to do? Don't you have other places you'd rather be? Don't you have other conversations you'd rather be having, other goals, other potentials? In other words, more satisfying things to get on with in your life now! (You will have to decide that question for yourself.) The fact is, many in the Silver Generation do not have the patience, let alone the time it might take to change attitude and behavior patterns. Simply stated, many entering that age are unwilling to wait for societal factors to catch up with remarkable advances being made in science, medicine, and technology to ward off the aging process. Hence, for many, the future is NOW! The question then becomes, "How do I deal with it?" Act defiantly!

A Model for Empowerment: *"Stop the World!"*; *"From Now On ..."*; A New Banner

So, if suddenly you find yourself being stressed out or saddened or downright deflated and depressed by what is being said to you, remember Anthony Newley's great moment in the play that ran on Broadway in the sixties: *Stop the World, I Want to Get Off!* Remember when the meek little lackey who carried the bags of the supposedly strong, genteel, snobbish "gentleman" (and now pretender) Cyril Richard, after enduring much verbal as well as physical abuse, finally put up his hand in a defiant gesture that is the universal signal of STOP—and sang out defiantly the magnificent line: "From now on, we're gonna do things my way!" The audience cheers the downtrodden lackey who had been the former acceptor of insults and sarcasm and jabs (and you name it) for defending himself at last!

The first part of that theme—"Stop the world!"—would be the slogan and manner I would urge this generation to adopt, where necessary, along with "From now on ...". What do you have to lose? A world, perhaps, you are not liking too much, that you may be liking less each day? What might you gain? A world filled more with the "you" that you want to be and for whom you have more self-respect. That means demanding, as well as asking, that this world move over and make room for you by providing an environment that embraces your worth, that is open to sharing your treasure house of the world within the self you are exploring. That is your right. You're really not asking for much, are you? Not asking for anything that shouldn't be available, but rather asking for something that will not only enrich your life as you enter that age, but most probably deeply enrich the lives of the society in which you live! Don't ever forget how very much you have to offer, no less than your total life's knowledge and experience which leads to a great deal of wisdom. You do not want to drop out of social situations; they afford you too much potential as an outlet for sharing and communicating thoughts and events, and giving and getting the enjoyment of being with those whose presence can make a difference. There is much to be gained in social settings. However, at this point in your life, as many of you have realized, you cannot and should not allow inappropriate and outmoded social behaviors to interfere with your rights and desires to be comfortable and full participants in the world in which you live. Such social behaviors negate the benefits you can and have a right to derive from social interactions, and too often, in such settings, you cannot contribute all you want. They can be stopped. If that means demanding that room be made for the social situations that can provide you opportunity for fuller growth and expression, that's your right! Even if you have to demand it; even if you have to age defiantly!

Well, men and women of the newly developing, assertive, and longer-living Silver Generation—this is your moment! And there is no backtracking. You must be sharp, you must be quick, you must expect those moments and deal with the situations quickly and firmly, gently if you can, defiantly if you must. I am further reminded of the lyrics sung by Anthony Newley in *Stop the World!*: "Just once in a lifetime/a man knows a moment/One wonderful moment/when fate takes his hand ....." Well, members of the Silver Generation: This is your moment.

By now, you know also there is simply too much at stake. Those moments may define you and determine how gracefully and with what dignity and integrity you enter this Silver Generation, as well as the extent to which you can spend your precious time exploring the treasures within yourself and building new hopes and dreams and quite possibly making contributions of inestimable value—instead of dealing with artificial barriers and social attitudes that lack substance. The path is open for your dynamic generation, so if you have to, demand it! Don't settle for less than you are, less than you can be! What else is new? You've been there before. Carving the world to shape yourself: The you, the person you want to be, is a right of your generation. So if you must act with spunk and age defiantly in order to attain that kind of world, so be it! Believe it! Empower yourself!

Why Aging Defiantly?

Aging defiantly—which comes down to a demand that society be considerate of the needs of others—may be not only a necessity, but also a most effective tool. That is not to say that kinder and simpler strategies and reminders won't work as well as harsher ones in warding off unseemly, intimidating social behaviors—and in the next section, strategies on both ends of the scale are suggested. It is the consciousness of what is happening and the understanding that what must be done, must be done by those entering that age—and if it can be done easily, fine, but if it cannot, then you will need to consider other, harsher strategies that work for you. You can handle it! Empower yourself! Therefore, aging defiantly becomes an important area of development for those entering that age. In a world that seems to thrive on intimidation, to the extent it does, the ability to manage intimidation with defiance and spunk should be seen as an essential tool to ensure the environment for your generation is one in which your enormous potential can be realized.

Maybe, some time in the future, society will understand better and act better, but for many of you, as for me, this is not really a very soothing thought at this stage of life. I have a dear friend—at least, she used to be a friend; as we got to that age and went off together, as we had done over the years, at every opportunity that came our way, she would say, "Oh, my friend is older than me," and she would take me by the hand. Her act and gesture clearly implied that I was not as swift as she and was in need of help as we traveled from place to place. Her acts and words placed me outside of the socially accepting environment; I thought I appeared needy. I felt suddenly intimidated. She would say such things as, "Shall we take the elevator? You should not be walking so many steps." She said it pretty loudly too. Not funny; maybe at some point it had been—when we were twenty, perhaps. Maybe I hadn't liked it then either, but I probably just smiled and let it go. But this time, I saw it differently. Did I ask for accommodation?

Or even if I did, wasn't there a discreet way for this friend to offer assistance to me without making me feel embarrassed, a loss of self-esteem, intimidated? And once that happened, I was stuck with that loss of self-esteem and confidence. The personal loss from that kind of situation is that you may not offer the thoughts you have; you may not be daring in what you might want to say or do—or as innovative or creative in your thinking as you might have liked. (It takes a supportive environment to be relaxed enough to share those types of ideas!) It simply might take too much effort. You may allow those conversations you were thinking about introducing to slide by. It simply may not happen unless you—AGE DEFIANTLY.

As for me, I lost that opportunity with my friend to change that situation: I did not heed my own advice to basically nip it in the bud. (Perhaps I had not thought of the importance of that yet.) And yes, my friend might have just meant to be funny or cute, but she should have known better. It was not funny; it intimidated me—and it was wrong. Friends have a duty to notice when they have hurt you; friends have an obligation to ensure that you are comfortable and not create moments that embarrass, humiliate, poke fun at you—and intimidate. (See the Michael Caine story that follows.) However, I am no longer willing to act as I had before, to let it go: The intimidating moment is absolutely no longer acceptable; I now know how much is really at stake. I need all the strength I have, and I need an environment that allows me to go forth into my potentially far-reaching future aspirations—starting right now.

So there are two aspects working here: One, if you are to go ahead with the pursuit of your life despite the natural changes that come with living, you will have to be firm and in control; you will have to empower yourself. Two, if you want to be listened to and not interrupted or made fun of or used as a butt of someone's unfeeling ego trip, you will have to age defiantly. So many situations come to mind: give it a moment's thought—and do not let the attitude of poor behavior patterns of others deter you: age defiantly. If you think you can't, think again. Remember, you empower yourself! If you are unsure, I suggest you read this chapter and the next with care, where I have spelled out many tactics and techniques that can be adopted fairly quickly; the art of intimidation management may be a little harder to understand—although I think not—but many strategies and techniques can be put to work for you as you make your way through an active and full life. The journey may be a daring journey, but it is one of a continued self-realization as a full-fledged member of the Silver Generation. Empower yourself!

The Consummate Artist of the Aging Defiantly Technique: (A Dialogue From a Late-Night Visit With Michael Caine)

I leave you with this instructive and illuminating story.

Recently, I saw the beautiful Michael Caine on a late-night TV show. Most members of the Silver Generation, I suspect, know him well: actor, author, raconteur—he has made our lives rich. Whether he has played on Broadway in a two-man show with Christopher Reeve or in a Shakespearian role, or as the debonair hero of *Georgy Girl* (which I regard as an earlier version of *Pretty Woman*), Michael Caine has been a favorite for a long time. Now a part of the Silver Generation, he has not retired; he has many goals and plans and was not hesitant about discussing a directorial role coming up, which he was animatedly speaking about the night I watched the show.

Nevertheless, the most interesting of all points this lovely man made was when he was asked by the host about the art of joke-telling—in particular, jokes played on him by others. He had an immediate and strong remark to make. With evident feeling and not-too-thinly veiled irritation and annoyance, Mr. Caine said, turning serious, "I don't like jokes played on me.... Oh, no! I don't like being the butt of jokes.... I don't like that kind of humor." And when the late-night host asked him what he did about that—without hesitating, he said that he looked the person right in the eye and told him, "I don't like that, don't do it again!" And as I recall, sheepishly with a twinkle in his eye, he added something to this effect (with wit and charm, of course): "I tell them I'll kill them if they do that again!" Of course, the punch line was in the vein of a joke: The audience had no trouble understanding that joke—or maybe Mr. Caine was merely imitating that earlier icon Milton Berle, whose use of that phrase, "I'll kill you" (which I'm sure many of you will remember), became a mainstay for *The Milton Berle Show.* But there was no question that Mr. Caine was serious about the diatribe on jokes told at the expense of individuals, especially him—and his silver hair left no doubt as to what generation he had entered. And in that short dialogue, he expressed something important for those entering that age: Don't tell jokes at my expense; I don't like it! I won't like it! I won't tolerate it! And I won't like you for doing that! So, dear friends, you are not alone; you have very visible, well-known, and much-admired and eminent members of your Silver Generation accompanying you on this journey to individuality with dignity, integrity, and spunk. Remember that as you set out to take charge—and do what you must to make this world your world, even when you have to age defiantly.

Take a moment out to reread, if you will, the opening paragraphs of this chapter. Remember that empowerment is what you give yourself. You empower yourself the moment you decide, "I will not allow this inappropriate behavior toward me." So go on saying it. You can not, you will not, and you should not deprive yourself of techniques upon which so much depends: living a life you want, respecting yourself, participating fully—and being able, without unnecessary hurdles, to carve the life that will afford you the most satisfaction and sense of worthiness. That is not too much to ask of this world, is it? For it is all you ask, really; no more, no less! You have a right to enjoy your life— and if hospitable social settings are important to you, as they remain for many, you have the right to demand courtesy, respect, and good manners (interesting how the poor behaviors fit into these categories, isn't it?). And if it means you need to age defiantly along with dignity, integrity, and spunk, then so be it! Empowerment is the moment you decide ...

If this Silver Generation is to take advantage of the enormous opportunities available, every single day, they will not want to abide the slow pace of social change: Aging defiantly, therefore, seems the most natural strategy and technique to bring about an expeditious change in the social environment that your generation must have in order to fulfill their enormous potential. So empower yourself, and move toward that glittering future that awaits you—now!

Chapter 13

DEBUNKING MORE MYTHS IV:

Intimidation Management

The slogan I would urge those of the Silver Generation to adapt would be "Stop the World!" from the hit Broadway musical of your time ... and in that moment of frozen time, assert, as the antihero who won our hearts did, "From now on, we're gonna do things my way." What do you have to lose? A world you are not liking too much, that you may be liking less each day? What might you gain? A world, perhaps, filled more with the "you" that you want to be and for whom you will have more self-respect?

Introductory Comments[11]

The most difficult of all aspects of the "get people off your back" syndrome is the handling of the intimidation factor. Sometimes, it seems as though our generation has raised this to an art form. Undoubtedly, it is a factor of life. Unfortunately, the Silver Generation has much

---

11 Intimidation, as I see it, is not losing a thought; it is not your short-term memory functioning sluggishly; and it is not really the moronic senility questions people ask to trip you up and show signs of losing it: "What did you eat; what did you do last Thursday?" Although it is a bit closer perhaps to the social interrupters and behaviors that throw you off balance, intimidation is in a world unto itself: It is a hostile act perpetrated on you (done to you) by others, more often deliberately, that interferes with your ability to function well in social settings. At this point in your life, this is not acceptable behavior.

179

to lose by succumbing to intimidation. This is not an area we may particularly want to embrace. Unfortunately, it is one of those areas that can result in devastating blows to the ego—made more fragile by time. Unless these hard-hitting put-downs are skillfully handled, those entering that age will have a hard time maintaining the dignity and integrity necessary to make the inroads waiting for them in this dynamic new age.

The term "myth" has been used widely throughout Part I of this book to refer to the fallacies of the criteria people use to indicate that some action or another on the part of those entering that age means that they are losing it, and further, to falsely create the impression and attitude that these criteria are indicia of lessening of mental faculties in those entering that age, which call for altering their patterns of living. I have exposed these myths as, for the most part, exaggerations of previous behavior patterns that can be compensated for without too much difficulty. Hopefully, by now you have been successful in applying a multitude of these techniques to ward off the assumptions that should not be made and the questions that should not be asked.

The intimidation factor differs from the myths presented in Part I of this book because in order to control and eliminate the effects, they require more than establishing a routine, more than a clever response; they require that you recognize what has happened and simultaneously take charge of the situation. Hidden under social amenities, they are, at first glance, not readily an inappropriate behavior pattern. After all, you have been experiencing them in one way or another in social situations for a long while. Maybe you regarded them as rather sharp, perhaps meant to be witty, but they can no longer be allowed to hide behind that disguise.

The intimidation factor is associated with behavior patterns people use to attempt to create environments that impede the ability of people to mentally function at their peak—your ability to both be comfortable and participate in the conversations around you; in fact, at times these "witticisms" make you downright uncomfortable, and probably have for a long time. But by now, you know better, don't you? You allow them to go by at your own peril. You now are astute enough to know they cannot go unchecked and also, hopefully, confident enough to feel you can tackle them because you have to, because you want to, because you will not suffer fools lightly.

Although more difficult to handle, the intimidation factor responds readily to strategies and techniques of coping that can be learned without much difficulty. In order to control the behavior of others toward you, this unfortunate behavior pattern may well require the willingness, ability, and effort to act defiantly and defensively. Like it or not, defiance, as stated in the previous chapter, may be the most effective technique to overcome the hindrance of the Silver Generation's pursuit of certain aspects of their dynamic new world. So you will need to recognize, react, and take action quickly as the intimidating remark or act is occurring.

For members of this new and dynamic generation who will have available both mental and physical health and stamina throughout much of their lifetime—which, as a gift from the sciences and medicine, should be very long indeed—this formerly bite-your-tongue acceptable social custom becomes more and more unacceptable as a social pattern, doesn't it? And because the intimidation factor is seen as a severe impediment to participation in social situations, whether intentional or unintentional, the behavior is becoming, for many, no longer acceptable as a social phenomenon (if indeed it really ever was!).

And so, if the social environment must be adjusted to make room for full participation of your new and dynamic generation, I am sure you will agree, the intimidation factor must be met and its impact minimized. So by now you know, the correct question will be: How do I accomplish it? How do I best handle it?

What Is Intimidation?

As a Supreme Court justice said in a famous case involving pornography, which did not exactly lend itself to an explicit definition, we may not be able to define it, but we know it when we see it. In other words, we recognize when someone has crossed the line. And so it is with intimidation! This new Silver Generation, larger in numbers and stronger in body, may not be able to exactly define intimidation for all circumstances, but you sure do know it when it hits you. Who among you has not felt the sudden sense of foolishness or embarrassment, or the faint flush or catch in the throat because words suddenly thrown your way are not what you had expected or anticipated? Who has not found it difficult, at times, to respond or perhaps has even stuttered trying to retain a proper response to a hurtful barb when unkind words or phrases are hurled at you? Ask yourself if you have not, at times, felt a pang of embarrassment or a flush of humiliation like the imagined sharp point of an arrow, or perhaps like an unexpected slap in the face? If you are honest with yourself, wouldn't you have to admit you have?

And doesn't it often happen in the company of people you least expected to be hostile, or often causing a sudden unexpected defensiveness to overtake you? Your defenses are down (more so the case as we cut back on our workload or retire and spend more time with friends and family). How ironic that in these circumstances at this time of your life, the demon intimidation rears its ugly head. You may bite your tongue; you may try to respond; you may even feel yourself getting angry. You should! Life should not be doing this to you—not now. And face it, when it happens suddenly, unexpectedly, don't you sometimes wonder if you are up to handling this situation I call the intimidation factor? By now, you should know the answer to this: There are techniques and strategies to offset this type of inappropriate behavior. Try defiantly!

You have too much to lose to allow this type of behavior pattern that is intimidating and curtails your talents and potential. Aging defiantly may just become a needed technique or tool in your arsenal of taking charge. It may not be for every one of you, but if nothing else, you should be alert to its repercussions and to some of the ways to handle these situations, because your life is worth it. Although a range of responses is suggested, from one extreme to the other, I must repeat, at the outset, the strategies that often work best are the no-nonsense approaches that demand members of this Silver Generation to age, not only with dignity and integrity, but sometimes also with spunk and defiance.

So in the next few pages, you will learn techniques to turn the unkind games people seem to delight in playing, especially directed toward those entering that age, into manageable situations. Whether done intentionally or accidentally, the results are still the same. Let me make it very clear that these so-called social amenities can be deadly to those entering that age, resulting in loss of esteem and confidence, and the deadening of the ability to participate in social situations of which you are a part. They are not to be taken lightly. Whether these barbs, jabs, smart remarks are allowed to continue in your presence is up to you. By the end of this chapter, you should feel empowered to put aside tactless behavior that may be preventing you from full participation in the social milieu.

Although perhaps more difficult to handle, fortunately, as with the problem areas discussed in earlier chapters, intimidation responds readily to strategies and techniques of coping that can be learned without much difficulty. I have given you a broad range of strategies and techniques to use in different situations. Not all of them will appeal to you, but there are a lot to choose from. I believe most of you will find techniques and strategies that are appealing to you. However, in order to control the behavior of others toward you, it may well require the willingness and effort of acting defiantly and defensively.

Defiance as a Technique of Empowerment

So let us explore the strategies and techniques available and also recognize that the changes that may get the most results in a short time, as indicated previously, are those that may well require spunk—and yes, aging defiantly! Sometimes, these methods will prove to be the most successful in the shortest possible time—because they are often effective the first time around. If this is your goal—and by this time, if you are still reading, it is—then you know the questions to ask are, "What shall I do? How do I accomplish this goal?" Defiantly! But you already know this.

By this point in the book, also, I think you will easily recognize that some of the topics from previous chapters are good starting points from which to handle these situations, offering a potpourri of examples to choose from, so you can shop and choose the ones that suit you best. I think, also, that you will quickly bring to bear your own tales of intimidation and woe—and begin to shape sharp defenses to bear on the situations you encounter. You are ready.

Avoidance Strategies and Techniques to Counter Social Intimidation for the Silver Generation

The "Word Supplier" and "The Corrector"
The Finisher of Sentences
The Look That Is Meant To Embarrass You
The Disrupter

Let's revisit the "miss-a-word" phenomenon—even if you've done it all your life—and focus on the person who is all too ready to supply the missing word, and look at how a supposed mistake, an error, or a momentary lapse can be handled by friend and foe. You make a mistake, use a wrong word, or pause for a moment looking for a word—yes, you may be a little slower (you don't need to be reminded it comes with the territory). Still, does someone have a right to jump at every opportunity to "assist" you—sometimes loudly enough so others take notice? I don't think so.

You just might want to take a moment to question their motives. Here are some benchmarks: a simple correction without interrupting the flow of the conversation would be friendly. A sharp, pungent, jabbing comment—causing you to lose your train of thought, or embarrassing you so that you feel a catch in your throat or take an involuntary breath—would surely be categorized as unfriendly. A seemingly kind response that nonetheless is cutting and hurtful might be one you will want to effectively handle as well.

I remind you that by now, you really know you have had moments like this all your life—and you have handled them or not handled them well. But at this point, you must do better—in other words, you can't really afford to let it pass, at least not let it pass indefinitely. Often the perpetrator, encouraged, will continue testing, emboldened to do it with more frequency. Alas, I must tell you it is bound to get worse:

Irritation creeps into the voice, or a tone that reeks of superiority or annoyance that says loud and clear to others, "Oh, she or he is doing it again!" And because you have now entered that age, that point might well be exactly what the perpetrator is trying to make. No longer acceptable! (Even if you were to attribute the person's statement to just poking fun—it's not funny to poke fun at those entering that age. Remember: The stakes are high; the remark, witty or funny, is at your expense.) The remark may well be taken to have a negative reflection on your ability, the inference being your thoughts or statement should no longer be taken seriously, because, well … you know. This is clearly not acceptable! Or more obviously, that you are not what you were. Cheap trick, don't you think? And not acceptable either! Any reason, with the skills and techniques you have mastered, you can't have a handy-dandy response ready?

The Word Supplier or Corrector

How to handle the person who is waiting in the wings to catch you looking for that word, or perhaps mispronouncing a word, or using an incorrect word? He or she can't wait, just jumps right in, makes a big point of it, makes sure everyone is aware of it; you know the kind: "unkind" in a nutshell.

Response: One word—"Whatever"! *Yes, whatever!*

(Accompanied by a smile or accompanied by a gesture of dismissal, better still!)

Then, quickly, without missing a beat if you can, continue on as though the person had never said a thing: do not acknowledge what the perpetrator is trying to do; pay absolutely no attention at all. I can tell you that it works! Many of you have seen this technique used effectively, if you think about it. An aunt of mine used this technique;

she used it from age forty, as I remember. Her reason: She was not going to let anyone interfere with the flow of her thoughts; she was not going to lose her concentration for a mere "word"; and she wasn't going to be distracted or, I suspect, going to give any attention to any person who would dare use this tactic on her. (Yes, she had an amazing sense of herself.) And by this act, she allowed her thoughts to flow on freely, no interruption, and made her would-be attacker/interrupter feel somewhat embarrassed or unworthy for not being noticed. This is really potent; try it—even if you don't need it at the moment, make a few trial runs and use a situation to take the opportunity to practice. (Yes, practice makes perfect and gives you confidence that you can do it.) Eventually, a habitual way of responding without too much thought will kick in, and far less effort will be required of you to respond to these types of situations.

Recently, I heard these words and saw that gesture of dismissal in an old flick I was watching. Of course, since it was old, the protagonist (female) was holding a cigarette as she and her companion were seated at a table. She simply flicked her cigarette (in her graceful fingers) across his face to the other side (one could almost see the ashes fall at the appropriate spot—think Bette Davis) and said (Yes, you got it!), "Whatever," while smiling condescendingly—and went right on talking. There was no room and no need for a further remark or gesture of any kind: It was a dismissal with a flare. It was a classic! I strongly suspect that my aunt did not need the protection at the time she started using it—but perhaps she recognized the long-term possibility (she was a total social being) and sought to avoid it, long before anyone tried it. Not many dared!

If you have one of those looks that you used to use to put people in their place—a stop-them-dead-in-their-tracks look—this is also a good time to bring it to bear and use the technique deliberately. My father-in-law, a sweet, gentle man, had one of those looks. He reserved it, as I remember, for just these situations: His look could be devastating. What it seemed to be implying was, "You've got to be kidding—for this you are interrupting me?" I loved it! His quizzical look and no response were some show-stoppers. I only wish I had adopted it earlier, but better late than never. If not now, when? Come to think of it, my father-in-law used this mannerism well into his nineties, and it remained just as effective at that age. No, it doesn't lose its effectiveness! (Now, I wonder, did he, and my uncles as well, pick up that gesture from a movie, too, perhaps—his generation was big on Humphrey Bogart?) Whether or not, they adopted it and used it effectively, especially for responses to members of the younger generation who dared create that kind of moment for them—I can attest to its effectiveness in warding off inappropriate behavior towards those entering that age. I was a keen observer.

Remember: People, friends, family, or acquaintances simply don't have a right to undermine you, whatever their motive, especially after you have entered that age. If they do, they deserve to be stopped in their tracks by the likes of a member of the Silver Generation aging defiantly, don't you agree?

The Finisher of Sentences

The finishing of a sentence for you can be deceptive at first because, at first blush, it may seem kind—until the allegedly kind finisher of your thoughts makes a cruel remark. (He or she invariably does!) So you didn't notice the greater and greater gusto and flair with which the act of supplying your word was done? And perhaps you found, as I did, that it was a bit too late for that moment? Check out what a supposedly dear friend did to me: We were on a trip together and she merrily supplied the word to complete my thoughts throughout the trip. I thought how nice and how close we have become to finish each other's thoughts—so we can move quickly from one subject to another, catching up, so much to share—relaxing too. But later, when we got home, this dear "friend" said to her husband in no uncertain terms, "I was beginning to worry that I might be moving into some of those 'senior moments,' but after being with Norma, I am absolutely high on myself"—and went on to give ample examples from the day's journey. Boy, hadn't I let myself in for that one? And wouldn't I be on guard for the next opportunity? You can bet I was! Best advice: Don't let it happen!

Responses

Some standard responses to keep in mind:

Please don't finish my sentences for me; I like to do that.

You can also say the following:

I am trying to think of just the right word, you know, the 'bon mot,' as the French say.

I know you are just as excited to be together and exchange stories as I am, but please: I don't like anyone finishing my thoughts for me—I'd rather do that myself, even if it might take a little longer.

Any number of similar retorts will occur to you, once you've decided you don't want this happening and that it is not in your best interest to allow this type of behavior, especially when you have entered that age. You might have to be more firm—especially if you have let it get started. But you can still stop it fairly nicely with a little punch or pizzazz.

If the person doesn't get it by this time, you will need to go into the defiant mode. Oh yes, even if this has not been your style, even if you don't already have it in your arsenal of skills you have used sometime in your life, if you have the will and the desire to stop this type of behavior, you will develop the skill. Why? Because it is important to you; because you don't like feeling embarrassed or intimidated; because it deprives you of an environment that is dignified and free of intimidation in all its manifestations; and because the stakes are too high.

The Person Who Has Gone Too Far: If you feel that the "finisher of sentences" is really at the rude stage (you let it go too far), you will have to be more assertive. In the situation described I should have used a "Stop the World!" hand gesture with my friend. I should have said to my friend when she made that remark to her husband, "If that's what you need to make you feel great about yourself, be my guest." She might just get the point. Or a quick annoyed or angry retort, "Cheap trick, my dear," might be called for, easy and to the point and generally effective. Some of you might want to add, the effective sound "tsk … tsk," along with a shaking of the head. (That often makes the childlike behavior seen for what it is!) Tables turned is fair play. Remember: It's your ego that is at stake.

One More Bit of Advice:

You can't always have the right response on hand, nor should you expect to; just know that there will be another opportunity. (There always is!) Once you get enough practice—and unfortunately, you probably will—it will become easier and easier as you become more proficient. It is, after all, only another skill. You can develop it; you can look in your storehouse—remember long-term memory—somewhere or other, you may well have had moments like this: try to draw on that memory. Either way, you will want to develop this defense. This is your life, after all, and you need to act on your own behalf for all of the reasons you know well by now. Try to remember who will reap the greatest rewards from stopping inappropriate behavior: You will. There is a time and place to act defiantly, and you will need to make that choice. Don't be surprised if, as you tackle these challenges, there are moments of empowerment. There may well be. Taking charge has its rewards.

One final word: *Never apologize for the natural change taking place as you enter that age:* It is not a weakness, it is a natural phenomenon. People should respect that, and if you are slower or more cautious or just one who looks for the exact word all the time (dumb habit at this point, perhaps), that's the way it is: You have a right to be who you are, with strengths and weaknesses, or "whatever."

The Look That Is Meant to Embarrass You

Those raised eyebrows, the holier-than-thou look, which seems to say, "Where in the world are you going with this?" or "What in heavens are you trying to say" (and heightens the effect by attempts to include others in the "put-down" look). Ever have this happen: A supposed friend or acquaintance or family member looks at you in this suggestive manner? I have! You might want to make note of this situation. A younger person who has been my friend for decades suddenly started to do this, and he went further—since I had let previous occasions of this rude behavior go on for too long. I told myself that I did this out of friendship and consideration for him: I reminded myself, those previous times, that he did not take criticism too well, and I did not want to offend him—until now. I should have known better—much better.

Here is what happened: Looking at the third party of our group, the friend blurted out while we were having a discussion one night at dinner, "I have no idea what she is saying, do you? Because if you do, tell me." I saw red, but clearly I also felt intimidated! I can't say I thought of all the things I could or should say, because I didn't. I muddled through it and left the conversation somewhere until I could think about this later. Obviously, I would advise not allowing a situation to get this far out of hand, as I did—but you live and learn, right? You can be sure I have vowed never, never to let this one go by again—would you? I am waiting for the moment, and believe me, I am well armed. And if you're thinking, who needs that behavior? You're right.

There are a few ways to go: Accept the abuse? (I think not, at this stage!) Make a joke? (He probably won't get it, but you can try.) Tell him off in no uncertain way? You will need to assess the situation: Is this rude and indefensible behavior in any situation? You might think so! Do you stand ready to lose this dear friend? A tough question, but I think, at some point, you do! The question to ask yourself is: If you allow this abuse to the ego and sense of self, will you be able to move towards your goal of aging gracefully with dignity, integrity—and yes, spunk? And don't forget that aging defiantly is oftentimes a necessary tool if you are going to achieve the self-respect you richly deserve—and this certainly looks very much like one of those times. You will have to decide this one for yourself. No one can decide it for you: It is hard to consider the loss of a friend—very hard—which is probably why I left it for such a long time without responding properly. I may have been able to respond in a more congenial manner earlier—but sometimes, life offers hard choices.

Other Responses

Let's look at a few techniques that might be good to have at our fingertips for moments like this and avoid the tough choices discussed above. They are difficult, and I don't discount the difficulty of getting your bearings, but here are some thoughts:

Response: The short phrase: *Give it a rest!* Said with the right look and intonation, this might just stop the behavior in its tracks. No more said; good response.

I had a dear friend (now departed) who used this short phrase, quite effectively. I am adopting it. I have found short, pithy, solid phrases often work as well: You can get them out quickly, you may be able to carry it off without showing you are upset, and they work! Here are some other responses you can try: You might want to try this response...

Response: *Return the look while simultaneously putting a hand up in a Stop the World!* manner to the innocent third-party onlooker. If your hand is firm, like a stop sign from a patrolman at an intersection—that kind—the third person will readily understand the signal.

Chances are, too, that other person is looking for a graceful way not to be involved anyway. Chances are you wouldn't mind if that third party came to your aid, but don't count on it. You may not need it; once a person is called on the above behavior, which is truly and overtly rude, the behavior needs to be stopped in its tracks. People seem to know when they have crossed a line and may well welcome a graceful way out. My friend usually followed his "Give it a rest" with a surly smile—but a smile—and that left a way for the perpetrator to back off.

A Few Catchall Suggestions

Here are a few other suggestions if the above doesn't work: Couple the look, and the hand gesture, if appropriate, with any of these remarks that you are comfortable using:

Perhaps you are experiencing a brain drain, dear (the "dear" is here to signal to the insensitive person that he or she might be acting in an inappropriate, infantile manner—and give you a chance to recover and get your bearings).

Well, it is perfectly clear to me! (Said with much annoyance and a cutting-edge voice; that is to say, sharp, clear, firm, slow, haughty—all you can muster—and accompanying gestures that seem natural to you: try a raised eyebrow.) The key here is to state your remark and quickly turn to the other person and another conversation.

Or Try One of These One-Liners:

I'll explain it again sometime when you're brain is in gear;

Obviously, your brain is on the 'pause' button, dear; we'll try again another time, shall we? (With the right tone, it will be obvious that the person is being childlike: He or she deserves it.);

I'll let you cogitate about it for a while (I got that one from a college president).

Perhaps your brain needs a jump-start.

Yes, some of these responses may be thought unkind. But rude, embarrassing, intimidating deserves rude, embarrassing, intimidating; it may be the only act in town—and you should not be the fall guy or gal. There is simply too much at stake. Choose: your pride or his (or hers)?

Caveat: Start talking about something else to another person—even if the conversation is about some plans for the next day you are thinking about at that moment. Leave absolutely no room for a retort. The conversation is closed—even if you have to say, "This conversation is over!"

The Disrupter

You are talking, and as soon as you pause for an instant or even a microsecond, the disrupter jumps in to challenge something you are saying, disrupting the flow of your intended conversation/point/statement, and winds up changing the direction you had intended to take the conversation. How frustrating—and how mean, because if a person was the least bit perceptive (wouldn't rule it out), that person should realize it might be difficult to get back on track. You may have been able to do this in the past, but as you enter that age, this is one of those things where your short-term memory may not be holding up as well as you'd like, and you must compensate. How? By—you guessed it—simply not allowing it to happen. But if you have ...

Response: As soon as the person is done with the disruptive interruption, go on ... as though he or she never even said a word. The trick is to hold your thought! Do not try to respond to the point that disrupted you, or even answer the question posed (even if you think you can give a quick response to dissipate the objection). Don't do anything, but continue your own line of thought, or it won't work.

A friend of mine has an annoying habit of always saying, "Can I just ask one question?" How do you say no to that? I have found over time that a seemingly simple question can be a potent interruption that can take you so far off course you will never wander back. Now, I say, "Please hold that question" or use the "Stop the World!" universal gesture, while simultaneously continuing to speak. Or I hold up the palm of my hand in the direction of the one who would interrupt (as I did when teaching a class long ago), or use the index finger (generally universal, too) to signify "in a moment" or "momentarily." After you are completely finished speaking, you can give these people the floor, if you please. If you are feeling dramatic, bow with the grand gesture of your sweeping arm—you have seen that many times (only if it works for you). (You never know when you might feel like giving that grandly exaggerated, but effective, gesture as a response.)

Caveat: Don't let the interrupter allow you to quicken your pace because you feel pressured by the one waiting in the wings to talk, and by your being made all too aware that you are preventing that person from speaking. The person deserves no respect. Speak as though you have all the time in the world. As a matter of fact, speak more slowly, for emphasis, so you do not lose your way, and maybe even make a point to the one who would seek to interrupt not to bother next time.

Other Types of Interruption Responses

Another friend of mine has the awful habit of jumping right in and saying, "But ..." and then going into his interruption, often lengthy and often moving in a direction I hadn't intended, after which I am in the position of having to say, "No, that wasn't the point I was trying to make, I wanted to say #1 ... #2 ..." How embarrassing to me, when I lose that second or third point because of the delay between my beginning and my own thought lost in the interruption.

For those who you believe are doing this on purpose to rattle you, because it's fun, because it gives him or her a sense of power, because you are, ahem, being tested ... for those, you must be assertive and quick on the draw: The hand goes quickly toward their face, the words distinct and sharp: "Let me finish!" That's it!

When you're done, you can turn to that person and say sweetly, "Your turn," with an exaggerated sweeping gesture. Sometimes a gesture is worth more than words—and you may find it easier to do. If you are really annoyed and irritated, you might not want to say a word: allow time for a poignant silence, and turn to someone else. The disrupter might understand, with any perceptive ability, what has been offensive to you.

Other Strategies and Techniques

If All Else Fails

Success Is Failure Turned Inside Out

The Art of Listening

The Art of Telling a Story

I think most of you will have gotten it by now and will be adding many of your own prized responses. As long as they work, they are the ones you should use. None of these are cast in stone; there are always other responses equally effective.

You can consider, too, simply not having serious conversations with some of the continual perpetrators of the above behavioral mannerisms: Maybe they are simply rude people or people you decide you might not want to interact with in these types of situations—not worth the effort. You will have to decide that.

When All Else Fails

If all else fails, or you are not in the mood to deal with all of this, but not in the mood to take it either, you have options: get angry or bow out or walk away, excuse yourself and leave. You can do it kindly:

"I have to get something" or "I have to use the facilities" or "I'll be back in a minute," or simply say, "Excuse me" and leave them guessing. Remember, you don't have to stay in an inhospitable environment— and some of the situations are hostile. You are strong, you have skills, you have respect for yourself, you can be assertive, and you can be defiant as needed. Do whichever is easiest at the moment, but don't take it. You have too much to offer to endure this nonsense. You can change it. Take charge!

Success Is Failure Turned Inside Out

When you fail, which you certainly will, from time to time (less often with practice), don't beat up on yourself: You are only human, after all. The jabs can hit you pretty hard exactly where you are vulnerable. It takes time to learn a new skill and get it down pat. You should begin to recognize "on" and "off" days. You should also know by this time that the object is definitely not to beat up on yourself. So what to do? You will know from earlier chapters that there has to be a quick way out of this situation too. Get a technique to handle it. My best one: I don't correct it. If someone says the word I should have used, I simply say, "That's what I meant." No explanation! No embarrassment! No fluster! I say it matter-of-factly and expect no retort from anyone. Usually, I don't get one either. Figure out your own best defense and try it. If it fails, try another until you succeed. (Sometimes, you just feel your way out of it—not anything you can do about it. Not anything you need to fret about, beat up on yourself for, or even apologize for. Learn to accept yourself! It's just the way it is!) You can also, if it bothers you and keeps happening, bow out of the conversation—the active part—and be a listener. You could say, "Wow! I knew I should have gotten more sleep last night," or whatever comes to mind. People love good listeners who don't interrupt, who appear to be listening, who show rapt attention.

Not honest, you say? Put it under the category of a survival technique. And besides, it's only a temporary aberration—for reasons medical- and science-minded people can probably properly explain.

The Art of Listening

A short story: When I was heavy into professional life, I sometimes found myself at meetings or gatherings with people from disciplines so unlike mine, I hardly knew how to begin a conversation. I generally muttered something—and then I listened. Yes, I listened. Here and there, I said something, generally repeating a technical word or concept I heard, but not much more. I was invariably surprised to find, at the end of our conversation, how many times the person told me how much he or she enjoyed talking to me, yes … that happened repeatedly. So perhaps when you put yourself in listening mode for the reason discussed above (you are not yourself that day), consider that you may just be giving someone a rare opportunity to talk. And be heard, or listened to, perhaps a dying art in need of resurrection.

The Art of Telling a Story

One final technique you might want to use: Here is an auto pilot approach that my partner uses a lot that seems to hold his self-esteem intact and make him unassailable. He merely tells one of his favorite five- to ten-minute stories, which he has told and retold many times. He knows the stories as though he was in a top Broadway show and the lines were imbedded in his mind forever: I suspect they are. I have adopted this technique.

If you have never used this technique, think about it now. It's relatively simple: choose a few stories—events from past or even present. Find ones that are funny, interesting, or dramatic from different times of your life; embellish them, sharpen them, repeat them over and over, practice them with dramatic flair if you can—and then go with it. Who would dare interrupt? You take the floor, you speak fluently, you speak coherently, with as few pauses as you can manage. The more you practice and use these prepared stories and events from your life, the more confident and comfortable you will be: good for the ego, too. (Remember, a tale or event told over and over again requires little conscious effort; it gets committed to memory.)

Who could ask for any more than that? Your ego will feel great—as will your self-esteem. Can't do it? Never did it? Do it now! Practice it as much as you need. It takes only a good story, good listeners—and deciding you are going to tell it, period. I never told such stories until recently. Then I started to think over parts of my life and chose interesting episodes or an event that had occurred—and I embellished it a bit here and there. So many interesting things have happened to you over a lifetime. Try it! You may just surprise yourself—and you just might enjoy the attention, too, while avoiding some of these intimidating situations; you may just start enjoying social settings again as you take charge.

Concluding Remarks

In short, this chapter has provided multiple ways to enable those entering that age to ward off those who would put unnecessary obstacles in the path of your generation's drive for recognition, dignity, integrity, and full and active participation in life. Those behaviors that prevent you from that participation must and will be managed by those entering that age: You have far better things to do and far more worthy goals to be achieved. At this time and place, with the help of science and medicine, you are entering a new world of limitless possibilities—a glittering one at that. Social patterns of behavior and outmoded attitudes that stifle this new dynamic generation—yours!—

and impede the growth, potential, and contributions call for strong and firm action. The stakes are high for the generation breaking new ground—yours. Many of you have already realized that you will be the pathfinders as well as the change-makers. And by now, dear readers, I hope you feel truly ready to take charge and chart your own course. You are already empowered and will continue to become empowered by the advances of science and medicine, and the dynamism of this Silver Generation. It is time to hear Emerson again:

> *The only person you are destined to become is the person you decide to be.*

> —Ralph Waldo Emerson

Chapter 14

MOVING ON WITH DIGNITY, INTEGRITY, AND SPUNK INTACT

You must be convinced you can take control of your own destiny as you enter the Silver Generation; as you make the decisions that affect the rest of your life; as you set your course on a path that is your choice; and as you move toward what may be the best of all life has to offer. In the end, as in the beginning, the choice is yours.

"Do not go where the path may lead, go instead where there is no path and leave a trail."

—*Ralph Waldo Emerson*

Entering That Age: A Personal Response

Yes, it can come together. I can personally attest to this. At the very moment I am struggling with the same short-term memory problems as you, my readers, I am writing this book. I have used, at one time, most of the methodologies and techniques and strategies I have suggested for readers to consider—and the others have come from or been corroborated by reliable sources or empirical data. I have taken a closer look at my strengths and weaknesses. (Yes, I am a better writer than a household manager; a better lawyer than an administrator—not rocket science conclusions, but nice to be totally clear about it.) I have tapped into that Personal Retrieval System, finding, to my delight, that I have a broad-based information system in storage. I have grown and continue to grow more confident in reaching for it. Confident, too, that if it is not right at my fingertips, it will come—not too long after I have set my search in process. Yes, my Personal Retrieval System works! I have used so many different facets of my learning throughout this book: PRS not only retrieves, it sorts and specializes and tantalizes. It is, after all, my Personal Retrieval System, my computer: my brain! It has stored what is important to me on this journey through life. I am pleased to say that the experience—although not without its difficulties—has been joyful. I have also learned to become more patient with my own retrieval system than I have ever been with a computer, as I have banged away impatiently on my computer to get it to work better and faster. (I am learning not to beat up on myself, too: I am learning patience to allow the pathways in my brain to receive and respond.) My patience has been rewarded—perhaps because I am still in such awe of the ability to access the memories stored in those brain cells.

Pulling out thoughts not played with for decades, knowing my life's knowledge and experience can be retrieved, not to mention skills like playing the piano and tennis, is a wonderful experience. Newer learning can come into play too: I recently did an enormous amount of research for a substantive article on classical literature and leadership which provided the opportunity to review many great classics studied so long ago, as well as to read some of the great writers I had always meant to but never did. I am finding that I can not only retrieve, but understand and integrate material long dormant. And I have been able to build on the data retrieved within myself: a true test, I think, of stored treasures still available to me after decades of disuse (or nonuse). Further, as I both read and discuss the body of work with a colleague, I take great pride both in the knowledge base intact within my PRS and the absorption of new material with far less difficulty than I had expected. This undertaking has given me rich new concepts and principles to play with after entering that age.

So I have learned that I can still learn difficult, substantive material, and I have gained renewed confidence in the individual analytical thought process and in the ability of the mind to expand as well. Science has begun to corroborate this ability of the mind to work in this way. Research studies on the brain are finding that potential exists for growth and development at all stages of aging. I have also read recently that although reaction time may slow down, knowledge—especially of world events and wisdom—may expand. Even the words I do not use every day, but need for these intellectual pursuits, I discover available and invaluable to me still. (There are some times when I prefer the more exact word, the word that enlarges and enhances—when, at that moment, the simpler word won't do.) I have begun to find, if I give my mind a moment more to work on my request, so to speak, the exact word I am searching for often comes to the forefront of memory. What joy this journey brings!

Does that mean that I am not struggling with the miseries of entering that age? On the contrary; at the very moment I wrote this, on the very morning, fragile fingers have dropped something again in the kitchen, breakfast has taken an inordinate amount of time to make because I decided not to follow my routine (just testing). But you can ask me what I had for breakfast and I will tell you, because I have the same breakfast every single day—except when I don't want to hassle with the stove and then I do a cold breakfast (a healthy one, though). I just asked my partner what day it is—so you know where I am on that. And I did not carry through on my own recommendation to put things exactly where they have always been—and so for the third day, I am still searching for something I need. (Oh yes, a new rule as I go along: If it doesn't show up for three days, and I can afford it, I buy a duplicate. There are more ways to skin a cat.)

Of course, if I had to choose between concentrating on mundane necessities of everyday life or exploring new treasures and thoughts, I would want to choose exploring the world within—my life pursuits are there, not yet accomplished. Although the satisfaction that I would get out of totally concentrating my effort on treasure hunts through my own trove of treasures is enormous, as is accessing data within my PRS, I cannot fail to notice or overlook or ignore the tasks, though mundane, that are important to my health and well-being on almost an everyday basis. I would probably get much praise from family and friends if I devoted myself exclusively to the performance of these everyday tasks: "Oh, she's smart as a whip; she doesn't miss a beat: names, dates, foods," I imagine they would say, and they would be happy that I am not a threat to myself or to them; of course, they would—so would I.

But I also know that any satisfaction I might get from completing these tasks on a daily basis, which would use up substantially most of my time and energy, would be greatly overshadowed by what I had left by the wayside—namely, myself. I suspect that you, dear readers, feel the same. Fortunately, you know, by this time, I do not have to choose—and neither do you! You can learn to utilize the variety of techniques and strategies discussed in this book—and find others as you go along as well—to ensure that those everyday nuisances that are nonetheless necessary get done in as efficient a manner as possible, leaving you free to be the only person you desire to be.

Fortunately, fulfilling the everyday necessities and fulfilling the self, as we have seen, do not have to be mutually exclusive. Many of the daily issues that formerly led to excessive concern, confusion, even panic no longer need be looked at that way, or have that feared result. With effort (sometimes a little amount, sometimes more), the everyday tasks that seem so time-consuming will fall by the wayside. In short, so many of the issues that concern you can be compensated for; so many of the problems respond to routines; so much of the things discussed throughout this book that are irritating and time-consuming can become habitual responses that take little or no thought, freeing time for more self-fulfilling thoughts. So are you beginning to get the picture? Simply stated: You can deal with it!

As you develop your strategies and techniques; as you compensate; as you acquire the confidence in yourself that they work and that you can handle them, you will free yourself for the life adventures of greater significance to you. And if you are not totally convinced, you might want to reread the chapters on compensation strategies and techniques and routines to handle the necessities of everyday life. Put the tools discussed to work for you; it won't be harder than many other things you have done in your life.

You will not have to abandon your loftier ambitions; you may not reach all of them, but you certainly can try to grab that ring: be daring. What do you have to lose? What you will gain, as you go through your silver years, is a rewarding life with integrity, dignity, and spunk—and a good life.

Three Other Stories

I want to share three very different stories of personal journeys. One concerns a dear friend and mentor who had entered that stage long before me and served as a guiding force; another is about a dear friend's husband who became my friend and, after he entered that age, found he had to struggle with physical problems that interfered greatly with his lifestyle—but manages, still, to be more than he should be able to be—and in the process is a continuing inspiration; and the third—well, the third is a story about continuing to climb that mountain. But first, I want to add a few remarks about the important effect of the health of the body upon the empowerment of the mind.

Effect of the Body on the Empowerment of a Healthy Mind

Just as an increasing amount of medical and scientific data has shown that those who use their mind retain a significant portion of it, probably for a lifetime, there is a fair amount of literature appearing out there suggesting that healthy bodies result in healthy minds as well. For example, studies are showing that maintaining an exercise routine, even as short as briskly walking thirty minutes every day, can result in clearer thinking and retaining flexibility and balance so vital to the functioning of your mind, as well as your body. I would be remiss if I did not point out the increasing body of literature suggesting that healthy bodies affect—greatly affect—healthy minds; healthy bodies affect mental health; oxygen affects brainpower; and exercise is a must for maintaining clarity of thought.

Researchers are finding a far greater relationship between mental deterioration and physical well-being than we would have thought possible. The potential effect of physical well-being on slowing, preventing, controlling, and—most significant for those entering that age—replenishing the mind (in what had been thought to be an inevitably aging brain!) is staggering. But once you consider this factor, again, I think you will find that it is not really surprising after all: It is a combination of common sense and serious research on the subject of relationships and interrelationships. See if you don't agree: Studies are indicating that disease (not surprising), illnesses (not surprising), and medications (not surprising) may even contribute to symptoms that characterize loss of memory, or brain drain (a colloquialism, but an interesting, descriptive phrase).

Again, not really rocket science, is it? After all, didn't you learn, somewhere along the way, that the important attributes of a human being are mind AND body? So are you really shocked to learn they work together in tandem, and what affects one part affects the other? I don't think so. Therefore, isn't it a small step to acknowledge that smoking, stress, disease, depression, and inactivity (as well as the other issues mentioned previously) may well contribute significantly to a decline in mental acuity as well? This being so—and it seems likely and makes common sense—doesn't it also follow that many of the social norms that have caused so many entering that age such excessive concern and, yes, panic about the so-called irretrievable loss of mental acuity are simply not true? I think it does; how could it be otherwise?

It also appears that members of the Silver Generation should be aware of the need for daily oxygen replenishment as well. What science and medical evidence seem to be revealing in the arena of diminishing mental acuity is that oxygen availability to the brain cells can, and often does, determine the brain's ability to maintain high levels of memory functions. Conversely, anything that takes away from that vital supply of oxygen adversely affects your mental faculties, e.g., smoking, environmental factors such as chemicals, lack of exercise and fresh air, disease, etc. The good news, stated before, but which bears repeating, is that some of the reduced brain cell function, that may well be caused by physical factors, can be also be restored when you return to good health—and start to exercise. It almost goes without saying that exercise, a walk in the fresh air (if you can find it), even taking deep breaths of fresh air through open windows on a good day can greatly assist in replenishment of oxygen to the body (try it!). All of these activities can minimize some of the causes related to memory loss and, in so doing, help in the clarity of thought process as well.

The importance of exercise, too, as a factor in mental health cannot be underestimated. Most people who exercise routinely have invariably touted the clear headedness as well as higher levels of energy they experience afterwards. Research studies are affirming this. Of course, those of the Silver Generation who exercise regularly (and those who do it sporadically) already know these benefits. I, for one, am always amazed when, after failing to get to the gym (exercising in the house does not work for me), I suddenly find myself reluctantly taking time to go to the gym. When will I remember, I always ask myself—as the exercise time is ending and as the evening is progressing and I find I have greater stamina and a clear head and can literally do what I want to do for hours longer—how important exercise is to me? So important, I plan to add exercise to my routine on a weekly basis and not deviate for a number of weeks, until that routine is so set in my mind, I will not be able to abstain from going without conscious effort. In other words, make a habit of it. If this Silver Generation is to derive full benefits from this wonderful period of health and longevity on the horizon, it would be foolhardy to ignore the instant, sustainable benefits from exercise.

How Do You Feel About Your Age?

Unfortunately, those entering that age tend to have more aches and pains. One only has to look at the ads on television to realize the extent to which products for maintenance of this and that, filling the airwaves, are directed to the audience of—you guessed it—the Silver Generation.

As you enter that age, you know there will be increasing physical challenges you may face that may certainly be unavoidable: illness, deteriorating bones and muscles, and so on. Your knee doesn't work as well, nor, for that matter, does your hip or shoulder, which seems to be giving you more difficulty with the passage of time. You may well feel like one dear friend, approaching a critical birthday, who remarked with both humor and sadness, "What is a twenty-three-year-old doing in the body of one who is sixty?" How about seventy-plus?

There is no denying that those entering that age tend to have more physical challenges to deal with; however, there is a tendency to greatly slow down and all but eliminate physical activity. In other words, you coddle yourself—it goes with the territory. So you stop doing this, and you stop doing that—as you try to get through the day without pain. Understandable, but not the best theory in the world: All athletes know (have you forgotten?) that unused muscles atrophy—they atrophy fast. Soon you are not running or walking as fast as you used to, or walking without a cane or a walker. I overheard a conversation at a lunch table a few months back between two older men, obviously friends for a long time—or they might have been relatives. I could not help overhearing. One said to the other, "I don't want to criticize you, but I am your friend and I think I need to tell you. Since you sprained your ankle, you have cut back on all your activities. You spend your day sitting and reading, or moving from one chair to the other. You've stopped physical therapy: You said it was too much of a strain. You go out to lunch once in a while. You don't venture out on a walk, not even with a cane. You know … if you don't use it, you will lose it." The other man would not budge from his position; he said, "I hear you; now let's drop it."

In view of all the current research studies being propounded on physical well-being and its relationship to mental processes, don't you think it would be foolhardy not to strive to keep and treat that body well—and when you have physical problems, strive to get over them, or to get back to the best shape you can, with help if you need it?

My friend, the one who was the twenty-three-year-old in the body of a sixty-year-old, is now more than seventy. He continued to play baseball until a few years ago. He often hobbled out on Saturday mornings; he hobbled back in, but he pitched ... and his mental health was great! As he got older in years, he underwent a few too many operations: rotator cuff surgery, knee replacement, and so on. Then he did physical therapy and returned to the game as best as he could—as long as he could. We can't all be like this; pain is pain—and it would be foolhardy not to back up, slow down, or do whatever is necessary. Ah, but there's the rub: "Necessary" is different for each of us. However, in view of the effect of physical well-being on your brain function, perhaps you need to consider pushing past the limits you may have set for yourself and, to the extent possible, getting back in the game as fast as you can—even if you make a slow start: Sitting at a ball game, climbing a few stairs, rooting for the team (jumping up to cheer!) may seem trivial, but it is a start.

I am seeing more people of the Silver Generation in gyms—the greying hair and silver white are strong clues of the generation they belong to. From physical therapy to massages, from working with sports therapists and trainers at gyms, they are working to overcome some of the previously accepted facets of debilitation and inactivity that for too long have been the hallmarks of the aging process. And they are succeeding. I even see people practicing how to get up from chairs without difficulty, without looking "that way," and learning how to strengthen arms, legs, and other parts of the body. The effect is better health, better looks, and a better general feeling about the self, AND better mental acuity. This is a new age: People in the Silver Generation are breaking these physical boundaries, too. And remember, there are exercises for every type of body, even those in wheelchairs: I see it all the time at the gym I attend—and no, there are not predominantly older people there.

This is definitely not the time to cheat on nutrition, diet, vitamins, or sleep—or other health factors that you know you should consider. This is not the time to coddle yourself. Of course, if you have an injury or deterioration of joints that will come into play in the decisions you make about activity. I am considering wearing a brace on my knee sometimes, but usually if I go into the sauna and hit the Jacuzzi with all the jet streams, I am all right. And maybe you need to use protective gear—that is a decision that you make with your doctor. Physical problems are what they are. But the point is you need to watch that tendency to stop moving your body and treating your body as a delicate object that might shatter if you move it—unless you must!

The contribution of the above factors to the well-being of your mind is probably far more than you know. No one knows your body better than you do! Use that knowledge to your full advantage. Don't skimp, don't overeat, don't starve yourself, don't beat up on yourself either. We can't all be like my twenty-three-year-old friend, in mind, if no longer in body, but for me, he has become a model. Treat your body well—very well—and you stand to be greatly rewarded for your efforts. Keep yourself in the best condition physically, and the rewards will undoubtedly be that you stand to improve your mental health along with it. Your goals should be to ward off deterioration, to maintain yourself at the point you are at, and to do the very best you can on a continual basis—no slack time for those entering this age.

So it might be said with impunity that healthy bodies are triggers to healthy minds; in other words, the health of your body may well result in greater empowerment to your brain. Keep that in mind! At the end of the day, you must be convinced you can and must take control of your own destiny as you enter that age, as you make your decisions, as you set the course for the rest of your life. This may well turn out to be your age, the Age of the Silver Generation.

Let me tell you one further story of another friend: my mentor and friend, who was considerably older than me. Once, we sat in an airport waiting for our call to board, and a lovely, well-dressed, poised young woman passed by ... she was at the stage I call "having everything." It was obvious: her looks, her confident stride, her clothes, her poise. "Oh, if only one could hold on to that," I remarked to my friend, who was well into her sixties (before this dynamic new age came on the scene), only to have her remark, without hesitation, without skipping a beat, "But inside, that's still who I am!" I have always remembered this poignant and heartfelt response. I have carried her words and that image around with me, and yes, that is the basis of the advice in the chapter. Now, closer to her age, I strive to maintain the inside, staying true to that look of a woman in her prime, in her thirties: It is for me I do this. I made a pledge to do everything I could to keep myself the way I see and want myself to be, for myself, and for my family and friends too, but mostly because it is my life I live, and time is important. I believe that is how many of you feel as well. Both of these friends' comments have served as guiding principles in my life and continue to do so.

I also strive to maintain my outer core in good physical condition. And if you are in the midst of a medical crisis or need to be on medication—remember that it can and will probably affect your thinking process, but it is also temporary and reversible. So remember:

don't beat up on yourself, and work to make yourself better and then get on with your life, in the best way you know how.

If you accept the fact that physical well-being affects your mental health and also may be responsible for many of the failings attributed to loss of cells (perhaps another hoax hits the road), then you can just, by your realization and changing your own habits, begin to mitigate the so-called hoax of cell deterioration. You, undoubtedly, now may possess more information upon entering that age than most people around you. Perhaps you will not be as hard on yourself, nor as irritated or as panicked as you have been in the past; perhaps also you will plan better and more properly—and to live the life you want, you will want to seek new knowledge as it comes to the fore and use it in the advancement of your worthy goals and aspirations in this new dynamic world you have entered. Now that you know what is happening, you will want to do everything you can to ward it off, to remain healthy in mind and body: The fulfillment of your self depends on it. This, then, appears to be on the horizon for you—and not the far horizon either.

So I close this section with a story of personal inspiration…

Climbing That Mountain: A Story of the Marriage of Body and Mind

In the beginning, as in the end, your goals should be kept in mind. A true marriage of mind and body can be in store for you. A dear cousin of my husband's, with whom he grew up and who, later on in his life, married and moved to South America, visited with us a few years ago: He and his wife and my husband and I had spent much time together in our earlier days. The time was dear, but we decided to find a suitable mountain and climb for a while. We did. But we did not set out, nor did we expect, to reach the top: The brochure said it was a moderate climb. We walked and talked—no problem here—and walked and stopped and had refreshments and climbed and talked, articulately and deeply and without those pauses, no problem here, some more. Hours passed as we leisurely made our way, stopping more than we would have at a younger age, replenishing our energy more often as well. But finally, finally, there was the peak. Joy filled our hearts and was reflected on our faces. The four of us stretched out on the slabs of rock: We laughed and took pictures each of the other. They, being younger, got down the mountain faster than my husband and me, but waited patiently, basking in the climb. That night, at dinner, our cousins said, "We did a wonderful thing today"—and we had. I had that picture that we had taken on the top of that mountain blown up poster-size; I look at it often—and the smile and joy of that moment is always renewed.

The point is, yes, you may have to set goals that are different and shorter and not as challenging, but does it matter, as long as they are your goals and ventures? Sometimes, though, even as you enter that age, even as you move into and through the silver years, there are those times you can reach that glittering silver mountaintop. And are you aware that research findings are indicating a far greater relationship between mental deterioration and physical well-being than we would have thought possible? The potential effect of physical well-being on replenishing the mind is staggering; a healthy body can slow, prevent, and control the aging of the mind. Pause to consider that as you read of this personal adventure.

Perhaps you will not climb the same peak, or beat your opponent as often, or walk as far, or walk without help, but is there anything more beautiful if you climb to a waterfall, or falling short of the mountain peak, if you stop with friends for a picnic lunch at a magnificent clearing, or park and go a few feet to a lookout where you can see mountains, and rivers, and valleys? I think not, and those I have spoken to and seen taking that walk up a gentler mountain, more like a walking path that constantly goes up and around, seem just as ecstatic when they get to a clearing and are dazzled by the height. The joy was the same as I remembered other hikers coming down from the top; their bodies seemed to exude joy (their conversations seemed buoyant and alive—must have been their physical exercise?). Perhaps, too, they were even freed from the pain of bodies in need of stretches and exercise (although they might have taken a few aspirin, when they got home). So life may still be a series of compromises, but what are you really compromising when you participate as fully as you can, when you participate in all that your life will allow, and when you are maximizing the health and welfare of your mental and physical selves to be all it can be—when you try your best to live fully on your terms, and you do? You must be convinced you can and must take control of your own destiny as you enter the Silver Generation, as you make your decision, as you make the decisions and set the course for the rest of your life.

You do have a choice in carving out your world for the rest of your life. As you reach that age and as you eliminate the nonsensical from your life, you will also be empowering yourself to chart your own life's course. It is time to expand your view of life to see more widely and more deeply. I believe your life can be truly enriched. I have thought about this concept throughout my years—and it has been a positive force, throughout my journey to reach the me I want to be, especially now.

EPILOGUE

YOU CAN DO IT

A winding down before you are ready, before you have done all you can and want with what you have, when it could be your best, your most productive time would be a waste—a waste of you. No generation (except, perhaps, in biblical times) has had such miraculous opportunities. The journey is yours to take … don't let anyone take it away from you: The twenty-first century may well belong to the Silver Generation.

Every day then a new beginning
every day a new opportunity
to move closer to the you
you know you want to be.

Within the self, there are other selves waiting
to be explored   this is the time to move on … [12]

A winding down before you are ready, before you have done all you can and want with what you have, when it could be your best, your most productive time would be a waste—a waste of you. You do not want to lose the opportunities being provided you to reach out to some of your long-awaited dreams and have them come true—these can be "the best of times"! Remember, you have scientific and medical

---

12 Except where otherwise noted, poems in this section are from *Fear, Trembling & Renewal: Poems to Age With* © 2009 Norma Roth

advances unheard of in any previous century supporting you. No generation (except, perhaps, in biblical times) has had such miraculous opportunities that are and continue to be opening—every day—as does this Silver Generation. So start with today—and never let it go.

You can do it! You have had many years of training and experience: use it—all of it. Look at it this way: You are probably smarter than your younger companions; you have more going for you; you have made it this far, and you sure are not going to allow anyone to slow you down. This is your last best effort, and anyone who gets in your way should be put asunder—figuratively speaking, of course. Now is the time! You know who you are, what you have achieved, what you still want to do: travel, write, read, play sports, or just be with good friends. Or work on projects that you meant to, but haven't yet gotten to enjoy. Enjoy the solitude that you never quite had enough of; perhaps take those long walks in the woods; sit by a warm fire; dine with dear ones; spend time in that log cabin, mountain house, or the beach; maybe teach, write, or be something you could not be when you were occupied with the kids, the work—the busy days. You aren't going to let anyone interfere with or take this time away from you, are you? You earned it! This, your last opportunity, may also be your brightest moment.

> *Life is a cycle, my cycle*
> *None the better, none the worse*
> *Life—my life is what I make it*
> *After all:*
> *I am the artist*
> *I carve my world—*
> *I will not sleep until*
> *The last breath is drawn*
> *I will not succumb:*
> *Greatness may be before me*
> *Not behind—I will not judge why*
> *I will live!*

So get those who would steer you in a direction you don't want to go off your back: gently if you can, defiantly if you must. Even with the best of intentions, others may try to impede or thwart or deter you from fulfilling your life's goals, the ones you set for yourself as you were growing up, past school days, marriage, parenthood; past those other phases of life. Now you have new goals; different goals; goals for the mature stage of your life; goals for your silver years, goals for the rest of your life. Remember: This *is* your life! Don't let anyone, including the now grown-up kids, the spouse, the well-meaning friend, the "tsk tsk'ers" ... pointing their fingers at you, interfere with your goals as you enter that age! These days belong to you. Make them special. This is your future!

And by all means, don't allow the lure of "Come, we'll take care of you at our dreamy sunset house—where you won't have any chores, where you'll bask in our care—where you won't have to make any decisions" tantalize you. Unless that's what you want! That's fine: It may well be the right decision—at some time—but not until YOU are ready! This life is yours, after all. Don't allow old attitudes to stop you from doing anything you want to do in your future; for these attitudes and behavior patterns, whether deliberate or inadvertent, have only one end: stopping you from doing what you might want to do—from fulfilling your life as you see it, as you have wished it, or want it to be.

> *Do I dare? ...*
> *YES, I dare!*
> *I will not settle for Hamlet's servant*
> *That will not do ...*
> *I will be Hamlet (or his sister) or—perhaps*
> *nothing—but at least I will try ...*
> *with my every breath*
> *'I grow old ...' so 'I grow old.'*
> *I will still say yes to life*

thrust my fears to the wildest winds
swirl and spin and spit
as long as there is a spark …
I will do it … I may not do it all
but I can try—
Life is in the trying
Life … is in the trying

What counts most, then, are *your* goals and *your* decisions! Let it be your decision for as long as you can. Let your world know your intentions: scream if you must. Sure, you must be smart and take into consideration your health, your abilities, your finances, and all the rest; that goes without saying—but you already know that. You are mature, not stupid! It goes without saying that you will be realistic and will take the required steps to provide for your necessities. But you also have assessed your strengths (and weaknesses) and know what you can do for yourself and what you need others to provide for you, which you will allow—as you need it. And you are smart enough to say, "That's not for me," or "I'll give it some thought when I'm ready," or "I am not in need of advice; I've worked it out," and when necessary, "Please, you are a dear friend, but get off my back!" The challenge is to assess for yourself, provide what you want, not what others (your family and friends included) think you should want, or back you into a corner to convince you what you need. Be wary before you put your hard-earned money away to pay for this "idyllic" care: idyllic for some—for you at some point, too—but you decide, when and what for.

Do not go gentle into that good night
Old age should burn and rave at close of day;
Rage, rage against the dying of the light

(From Do Not Go Gentle into That Good Night by Dylan Thomas)

That sword of Damocles will not fall on the head of a member of the Silver Generation unless you allow it to do so; there is too much at stake to let that happen by default. While your friends and acquaintances as well as your children look for "the signs," let them see other signs! Let them see you. You really do have a choice; you really do have the skills, abilities, and so much more, especially when you reach for those treasures that are within and without and tap into that Personal Retrieval System.

I have things to do
songs to sing
poems to write
photographs to take
life to live ...

The photo will be of ice
frozen white, cold
yet beautiful—
exquisite delicate form and shape

The poem will be of
infinite possibilities
fulfillment of promises
and potential long known
and yet to know ...

The song will be of myself
melodies collected
over a lifetime...those
known to me and also
those yet to be known

the song will be of myself
the poems will be of my heart
the photographs of my choice
the life to live ... mine ...

I have things to do!

I am convinced that for this dynamic generation—and I am utterly convinced it is dynamic—there are no barriers except the ones you make for yourself; there are no limits to how far you can go or where you will go except the limits you place on yourself. I do know that unleashing the knowledge within the self has not yet been explored to the extent it should, but it will be. The time has come for those of us who have entered that age to open wide those doors.

If you have understood the message of this book, it is that your generation is at the beginning of a new age and that you will be the leaders, the trailblazers, and pathfinders. You will be more ready, willing, and capable of taking charge, to join with others in your dynamic new group to clear a path for the adventures and fulfillment that are already waiting there—and those gifts that wait for you in this promising new century.

A few years ago, a newspaper in New Hampshire had this to say about a candidate running for Congress:

We think age seventy is a good age to run for Congress ...

That person was a dear friend; he did not win, but he tried and along the way he met people with similar attitudes towards aging and planning full and good lives based on individual interests and talents well into their later years, past seventy. When this candidate spoke at a large veterans function, he discussed Iraq and the concerns of the young soldiers there, their fears, and hopes, and dreams that would undoubtedly change because of the harsh experience of war.

I watched this audience of a few hundred men and women. This candidate recounted the experiences of his father and uncle in World War II, the young families left behind, the change in lives; and later, when he ended his speech (which had, somewhere along the way, become an intimate talk with friends in this crowded auditorium), he said to his friends, "This country still needs you."

There was an audible silence, followed by deafening applause. Clearly this group, Silver Generation all, was ready to serve in new and important ways. Who could understand better than these veterans the adjustment to life awaiting our new group of men and women coming home? I could see their minds working; new plans being made, new goals being set; they readily accepted the challenge. I could see it in their eyes and in their gait as they walked out, murmuring to each other in expectation of fulfilling the goals they were setting. New Hampshire is a state of hardy stock, where parents built log cabins for their families after working in the lumber mills—where life continues actively until it ends. No wonder our newly retired Supreme Court justice, David Souter, plans to return to the house his grandfather built, where, as I understand, the tables hold books on top of books waiting for him. And I can bet there aren't merely books on law. Life, as Erik and Joan Erikson and Helen Q. Kivnick described it in *Vital Involvement in Old Age,* has many phases, and getting old is simply another stage, and it does not stop when one enters the last stage: What is called for are new goals, new lives, new objectives: daring, some might say, but more natural in the scheme of things, more and more will say. As the Eriksons said: "Growing old can be an interesting adventure and is certainly full of surprises." Yes indeed.

Let that be you as you go on this bold new adventure and blaze the trail of the Silver Generation: make it glitter; make it sparkle; make it the best of you! And live to the fullest the wonderful life you have in store: an exciting and exhilarating journey filled with the greatest potential that the world has ever seen. So ...

Live to the full the joys of age as youth
But don't forget a basic truth
All your life won't mean a thing
If you lose the sparkle of that silver ring.

(Adapted from an unpublished poem by Sidney Jackman, 1954)

And with this longtime favorite:

Grow old along with me
the best is yet to be
the last of life
for which the first was made

Youth knows but half
…

(from *Pippa Passes* by Robert Browning)

APPENDIX

AGING DEFIANTLY

TEN TIPS TO KEEP PEOPLE OFF YOUR BACK

Introductory Remarks

This appendix deals quickly with the primary examples one hears about those "entering that age" (See: Entering That Age, Chapter 1) that signal you can no longer be left alone because you might leave a pot boiling on the stove, or you lose track of dates, time, and places. Members of this new dynamic Silver Generation, who have begun to feel concerned that those peering eyes, those questioning looks might be indicative that you are losing it, can learn these few simple tricks, and will find yourselves saying "Hogwash!" to those who would be so quick to put you out to pasture. Most importantly, those who feel, or have begun to feel, they have entered that age can learn that by simply changing a routine or adapting some strategies and techniques to compensate for the natural changes that are a part of life, they can ward off those who would be so quick as to deprive them of their independent lifestyle. You will wonder why you never thought of them yourself and why others never brought them to your attention. This is to help you wonder no more. While all of these areas are discussed more fully in the beginning chapters of this book, as well as other issues important to those entering that age, these ten tips give you a quick way to stop wondering, start handling, and get on with your life. This new dynamic Silver Generation has a great deal of living yet to do.

Ten Tips to Keep People Off Your Back

1. So You Left the Water Boiling

The cardinal sin: *He'll leave the water boiling and burn the house down.*

THE CARDINAL RULE: DON'T LEAVE THE KITCHEN UNTIL YOU ARE DONE.

So, you leave the water boiling on the stove and don't remember that you did it, if you leave the room ... what to do? Run for help, call the nursing aide, go into—heaven forbid—a nursing home? Think, for a moment, would this happen if you had stayed in the room? I doubt it! Simply DON'T LEAVE THE KITCHEN UNTIL YOU ARE DONE! Guaranteed, you will not forget to turn off the pot if you stay in the same room. Your senses are very strong tools; let them work for you! Try it; what do you have to lose?

2. Now Where Did I Put that ... Anyway?

The cardinal sin: *She can't find anything, she'll lock herself out of her house, or he'll never get to where he's going, he'll be looking forever.*

THE CARDINAL RULE: DON'T PUT THINGS IN DIFFERENT PLACES.

Don't put things in different places than you have always put them: No matter how much better or safer or nearer you may think a new place is, it isn't going to work. Put the darn thing where you always have, or you will be hiding it from yourself, and then have to go on one of those embarrassing hunts or painfully, under pressure, try to reconstruct your steps. Just use your old tried-and-tested places—even if you travel—always!

3. Why Did I Come Into This Room Anyway?

The cardinal sin: *He goes up and down a hundred times a day to get something and never remembers what he went for!*

THE CARDINAL RULE: STOP! TURN AROUND, WALK OUT OF THE ROOM, AND MARCH DIRECTLY BACK TO WHERE YOU WERE BEFORE, AND WAIT.

Try this little technique and see what happens: You come into the room and can't remember why ... STOP! TURN AROUND, WALK OUT OF THE ROOM, AND MARCH DIRECTLY BACK TO WHERE YOU WERE BEFORE, AND WAIT. See how long it takes to remember! Yes, you will remember, especially if you don't block yourself by berating yourself! When you get good at this and trust yourself, you may well find you remember sooner; then when you get really good, you may just have to pause a moment—and lo and behold .... (You knew this already, didn't you? But perhaps you hadn't thought of it as a technique—or classified the technique as a strategy—well, do it now.) It works!

4. Why Can't I Remember That Word?

The cardinal sin: *She stumbles over words; or you know, he used to be so fluent and now ...*

THE CARDINAL RULE: A FIVE-AND TEN-CENT WORD WILL DO!

The question is not why you can't remember that word, but what other word might readily come to mind that will do. When the word you want suddenly doesn't appear, use another; it hardly matters which: the simpler, the better. A five- and ten-cent word is perfectly all right in conversation: you aren't trying to be a Rhodes scholar—just use any old word that comes to mind! Nine chances out of ten, it will work in conversation!

5. What Did You Eat for Breakfast (or Lunch) Today ... or Yesterday?

The cardinal sin: *He can't even remember what he had for breakfast or what day it is ...*

THE CARDINAL RULE: SWITCH THE SUBJECT AND OTHER TECHNIQUES

Switch the question around: "What did *you* eat for breakfast today?" Quickly follow up with comments on this profound subject: "That sounds delicious. Do you go out to eat much? Did you go out this weekend? Are you planning to?" Or you can follow up with: "Let's go out sometime soon"; you get the point. You can stay with this indefinitely: "And lunch; did you have lunch? Are you dieting? How do you watch those calories?" You get the idea!

When or if the question gets back to you, HAVE A STANDARD

ANSWER: "My foods are fairly humdrum these days, not worthy of talking about," and repeat an invitation to dine together soon. The Switch Theory can be useful in so many social situations. Try this theory; it really works.

6. What Did You Do Today? Or the Wide-Open Question: What's Up?

> The cardinal sin: *This is often a test of memory for those "entering that age" by well-meaning (?), generally, relatives to determine whether your mind is working in the "present".*
>
> THE CARDINAL RULE: DOUBLE SWITCH Á LA MARTY: "NOTHING MUCH, WHAT DO YOU WANT TO DO?" Or, like to talk? Try the Cyrano approach (Act I, Scene IV).

To the "What did you do today?" question, use a variation of the Switch Theory and Marty Approach: "Nothing much. What do you want to do?" To the "What's up with you?" question, same approach: "Nothing much. What's up with you?" Then come to a dead stop. People tend to fill in the gap of silence; let them go on talking.

7. Did You Hear the News Today? Or What Do You Think About What Happened Today?

> The cardinal sin: Report to the world, "*She didn't even know that ...*"
>
> THE CARDINAL RULE: WHEN EXPECTING COMPANY, BE PREPARED! I HEARD THAT WHAT DO YOU THINK ABOUT THE SITUATION?

Boy Scout/Girl Scout: When expecting guests, be prepared: turn on the idiot box while you are going on with your chores and preparing; you can take in the day, the date, and the allegedly important news that television fills your ears with these days. (You can skip the gore and details of the current TV tabloid, just enough so you are in the know.) And then, when your questions come, you can spring it on them: "Isn't it terrible that …? Isn't it…? Did you hear …?"

Point of information: The public radio broadcasts are often a wonderful source of news and often intelligent discussion about a topic in which guests from all over the world, depending on the issue, give their point of view: stop for a moment and take in a bit and use it as a discussion, both current and interesting, if you are so inclined.

8. What to Do When the Mind Wanders

The cardinal sin: *You know the problem here: He can't keep his mind on a subject or thought for more than …*

THE CARDINAL RULE: HAVE A PREPARED RESPONSE: *I WAS JUST THINKING* PREPARE A STORY, OR EVENT, OR SUMMARY OF BOOK OR ARTICLE …

Any number will do: The trick is to have a conversation ready, and when you are called on for not paying attention or not knowing at what point the conversation you were supposed to be listening to is, go into that prepared text. Have a ready conversation: "Oh, I'm sorry … I was just thinking …"

The point is to have a real conversation ready: There are things you think about: people/ideas/books/places/nature; make a list. When your mind wanders (and we all do this, no matter the age), have a good conversation ready—one you would like to discuss. An extra benefit is returning to the art of conversation. Keep it going, too, for as long as you can—even if your asker of this question gets fidgety and seems to be looking for a way out; stick with it ad infinitum—perhaps he or she will get the point if you do this often enough and not be so quick to make such a mean remark. (And it is a mean remark.)

9. What to Do When Someone Interrupts Your Train of Thought

The cardinal sin: *He keeps forgetting what he wants to say …*

You may well lose your train of thought when you are interrupted more frequently and leave yourself open to those looks, the shudder-producing shaking of the head, or even whispered remarks that you just happen to hear like, "She loses her train of thought so easily; he's not as swift as he once was, he strays off …"

THE CARDINAL RULE: DON'T LET YOURSELF BE INTER-RUPTED!

Don't respond. Use the eternal full hand "Stop" gesture or point a finger towards the perpetrator and say, "In a minute," or simply say, "Whatever," and continue on as though nothing whatsoever had been said of importance to stop you from moving on. Don't respond. That is the point … even if you think their motives are pure. It will not serve you to allow that interruption. Yes, it works!

Often, the loss of the train of thought is due to the rudeness of others, ready to interject a thought that takes you away from your premise, by throwing in a phrase that is not at all on point, supplying a word that may or may not be appropriate for what you started to say, putting you in a position where you must hold on to your thought and also where you intended to take it—that is not an easy task, and it is rude for people to interrupt! NO, DON'T LET THEM GET STARTED: DANGER LURKS HERE.

10. Who Is the President of the United States? Who Was the President in …? Who Is the Leader of England, Russia …?

RESPONDING TO MORONIC SENILITY TEST-ING

The Cardinal sin: She doesn't even know who the president is.

THE CARDINAL RULE: WHAT? YOU DON'T KNOW? YOU BETTER SEE A DOCTOR QUICKLY!

I call these types of questions moronic senility testing, and they deserve this or any similar response that you devise. Unfortunately, once you have entered that age, people don't seem to be able to resist this incessant, rude, and moronic testing for indications of senility, which are more often than not absurd. Be prepared. Start thinking: You have been around long enough to respond sarcastically or with annoyance or sweetly but with venom or graciously, solicitously, and so on. Senility testing is wrong! (A good model for further types of appropriate responses to moronic questions is *Cyrano de Bergerac* (Act I, Scene IV).

Postscript

The question this century will answer is how much of the aging process will actually be preventable. Predictions are for "a massive increase in life expectancy" as well as "radical extension of life-enhancing technologies." Just how much replacement, repair, regeneration is anyone's guess, but a whole range of sciences is working on our behalf to maintain us, sustain us; one bold researcher said, "We are in serious striking distance of stopping aging." Will you see it? Will it come in your lifetime? Maybe so! It is an exciting time to be a member of the burgeoning numbers of those entering that age, whom I have called the Silver Generation. As I am going to press, the Harvard Medical School has sent me two leaflets: "Living to 100, What's the Secret?" and "Preserving and Boosting Your Memory." What an exciting world for the new dynamic Silver Generation to be entering, filled with promise, with hope, with potential for limitless opportunities: Eat well, live well, exercise. Exercise both your body and your mind … live and be healthy! Your time is NOW! And above all, age gracefully with dignity, integrity, and spunk intact, and when necessary, age defiantly: Do not let anyone take from you the promise that is unfolding. Hold these thoughts that they should give you motivation and confidence for what you need to do now to ensure that your life moves along as you wish it to. Dream big and dream now: This is your time, the Age of the Silver Generation.

Acknowledgments

This is a short bibliography, rather an acknowledgment of some of the materials I have found fascinating, helpful, and exciting in the pursuit of my theme. There is an abundance of material out there; every day there is more on the wonders and advancement in the field of the aging brain and body.

I owe special thanks to the following publications for their wise insight into the world we have entered that will allow this dynamic, new, and growing Silver Generation to become part of a new world, so that the promises of this new century can indeed be fully and completely appreciated, and those entering that age can be full participants in an era that is fast becoming, along with the Age of Biology, the Age of the Silver Generation.

Special thanks to:

Society for Neuroscience (SfN). "A Primer on the Brain and Nervous System." (They publish the weekly *Journal of Neuroscience*.) I am especially grateful for their efforts to promote public understanding and general education about the nature of scientific discovery and the results and implications of the latest neuroscience research.

For further information on the various discussions herein on scientific advancements, see, for example, the following: *Harvard Magazine*, "Neuroscience Frontiers: Probing Brain Cells" (January–February 2009 and May–June 2009); *The Pennsylvania Gazette,*

"Blueprints for a New Biomedicine" (January–February 2009), *Scientific American*, "Mind and Brain" (February 2009), and others.

I also want to give special thanks to the study papers and fact sheets that are readily available from many universities doing landmark work in the field of human development; regenerative biology; and repair, replacement, and regeneration from cells and cartilage to body parts and prosthetics. I am indebted to the following for making their papers available:

Brown University Fact Sheets: "Bridging the Gap Between Man & Machine" (August 27, 2008), includes limb lengthening, robotics, and neuroprosthetics.

Cornell University Fact Sheets: Bridging biology, human medicine, and engineering; micro- and nano-biotechnology (building micro-scale devices with interacting cells to form different tissues to predict the body's response to cocktail therapies for treating cancer); biomedical mechanics (leading to the development of artificial hips and knees); and molecular, cellular, and tissue engineering scaffolds to re-create certain functionalities of the extracellular matrix surrounding cells in the body (these may be implicated in the regulation of heart valve development, blood vessel function, and tumor biology).

It should be noted that major universities such as Harvard and Cornell have added and continue to expand graduate and undergraduate concentrations in human development, disease, and regenerative biology. The universities are also integrating sciences so that bioengineers can more and more draw upon and interact with others in the fields of medical science, physics, chemistry, computers, and more.

Erikson, Erik H. *The Life Cycle Completed. Extended Version.* With new chapters on the ninth stage of development by Joan M. Erikson. New York: W. W. Norton. 1997.

Erikson, Erik H., Erikson, Joan M., and Kivnick, Helen Q. *Vital Involvement in Old Age.* New York: W. W. Norton. 1986.

About the Author

Norma Roth has published a number of poetry books for the mature audience written from a personal perspective and dedicated to the last phase of life. In *Scenes From a Summer House,* she discovers there need not be boundaries between time and space, between beginnings and endings, while in *Fear, Trembling & Renewal* she explores the theme of finding a way "to see the world anew" when the "snow begins to fall" and accepts the dare to say "YES!" to life. In her first full-length book *Aging Gracefully with Dignity, Integrity & Spunk Intact: Aging Defiantly,* Ms. Roth seeks to paint a larger landscape for those moving into their silver years, whom she calls the dynamic new Silver Generation. Included in her new book are "Ten Tips to Keep People Off Your Back."

The author sees this new generation as robust and intelligent, highly skilled individuals, moving into their senior but not their vegetative years. Old concepts are out; new concepts are in as scientific advancements outpace social attitudes. She sees this generation as trailblazers and pathfinders. An age of fullness, an age of new parts for the body and expanded abilities for the mind for almost an entire lifetime awaits.

To succeed in the achievements being made possible by far-reaching science, medicine, and technology, outmoded barriers and hurdles that stand in their way must be met head on—allowing the new, dynamic group to be *Aging Gracefully with Dignity, Integrity and Spunk Intact* and, yes, *Aging Defiantly*. This book charts that course. The author, a member of the Silver Generation, invites you to take this amazing journey with her. Ms. Roth truly believes this will be the Age of the Silver Generation for whom the twenty-first century will afford endless opportunities for new dreams, new plans, and new paths.